Taste of
MAUI

Taste of
MAUI

Favorite Recipes from the
Maui Culinary Academy

Taste of
MAUI

Favorite Recipes from the
Maui Culinary Academy

Edited by
Chris Speere
with

Bonnie Friedman,
Corinne Domingo,
and Karen Lofstrom

Photography by **Steve Brinkman**
Artwork by **Ed Lane**

MUTUAL PUBLISHING

*To the students of the Maui Culinary Academy,
with thanks for your passion to learn and
develop as leaders in our dynamic and
challenging industry. To our inspiring chef
instructors, who lead our students through
uncharted waters, and encourage a daily
commitment to excellence as a recipe for success
in and outside of life's kitchen.*

Copyright © 2008 by Mutual Publishing

Library of Congress Cataloging-in-Publication Data

Taste of Maui : favorite recipes from the Maui Culinary Academy / edited by Chris Speere ; with Bonnie Friedman, Corinne Domingo, and Karen Lofstrom ; photography by Steve Brinkman ; artwork by Ed Lane.
    p. cm.
  Includes indexes.
  ISBN-13: 978-1-56647-884-7 (hardcover : alk. paper)
  ISBN-10: 1-56647-884-7 (hardcover : alk. paper)
  1. Hawaiian cookery. 2. Cookery--Hawaii--Maui. I. Speere, Chris. II. Friedman, Bonnie, 1951- III. Domingo, Corrine. IV. Lofstrom, Karen. V. Maui Culinary Academy.
  TX724.5.H3T3775 2008
  641.59969--dc22
                    2008033143

ISBN-10: 1-56647-884-7
ISBN-13: 978-1-56647-884-7

Design by Courtney Young

First Printing, September 2008
Second Printing, March 2010
Third Printing, February 2012

Mutual Publishing, LLC
1215 Center Street, Suite 210
Honolulu, Hawai'i 96816
Ph: 808-732-1709 / Fax: 808-734-4094
email: info@mutualpublishing.com
www.mutualpublishing.com

Printed in Korea

TABLE OF CONTENTS

FOREWORD

From one of the Best Islands in the World, according to *Condé Nast*, I am pleased to introduce the latest contribution to the field of gastronomical and culinary literature. This project was inspired by the faculty leadership at our Maui Culinary Academy (MCA) as part of the University of Hawai'i – Maui Community College. We congratulate our MCA Program Coordinator Chris Speere for his vision and persistence, and we thank our MCA community partners Bonnie Friedman, Steve Brinkman, and Ed Lane for their generous support and creativity as well.

When each recipe is faithfully replicated in your kitchen and home, you will share in our college and community's continuing celebration of creating culinary experiences that are visual and tasteful feasts. If you are ever on Maui or are part of our island community, we invite you to the Maui Culinary Academy on our Kahului campus for a wide range of choices in cuisine. Our faculty educate and train our students in the culinary arts. Their products are designed, prepared, and served from our kitchens, confiserie, bakery, various stations (Farm to Table, World Plate, Paniolo Grill, Raw Fish Camp [sushi bar], Campus Grill, and Patisserie), and our gourmet dining room, the Leis Family Class Act Restaurant.

I know you will enjoy the culinary recipes and the tasty dishes that follow. I also hope that you will join us in our Pā'ina facility, home of the MCA, to experience how the chefs of tomorrow are being trained today.

Mahalo nui loa,
Clyde M. Sakamoto
Chancellor
UH Maui Community College

ACKNOWLEDGMENTS

A heartfelt appreciation to editor Bonnie Friedman, who has captured the essence of our program in words and recipes as no other person possibly could. Her guidance, candor, and patience to see this project through long after her duties were complete was no easy feat.

Thank you Ed and Diane Lane, who gave their time, care, concern, and artistic talents to ensure the success of our book.

To Bennett Hymer, Courtney Young, and the Mutual Publishing team for believing in our program, promoting our vision, and allowing us the freedom to preserve the integrity of our recipes.

Thank you to photographer Steve Brinkman for his creative touch, unlimited patience, and his skill in capturing our food in such a beautiful manner.

Thank you to Chef Tom Lelli for taking the time to lend his support to this book, test recipes, and serve as food stylist.

To Corinne Domingo and Karen Lofstrom, both of whom were indispensable in the final editing process, for bringing the book to completion, and assisting us in show-casing the Academy as a world class culinary school.

To the members of our Maui Community College campus—far too many to name—who provided encouragement every step of the way.

And to the talented Chef Instructors of the Maui Culinary Academy who from the beginning provided unwavering support and the creative recipes contained in this book.

INTRODUCTION

A meal at a great restaurant is a marvelous extravagance. The décor is chic, the service is attentive, and the food not only tastes divine, but it also looks beautiful. It is composed on the plate (plated) with care, balancing shapes, colors, and textures. The chef has carefully selected all the ingredients on each plate to create a symphony of tastes.

Is it possible to duplicate this experience at home? It's not impossible, but it can be challenging. A restaurant has the ability to buy the best ingredients in the marketplace. A restaurant kitchen is well-equipped, and run by a team of trained professionals who cook and strive for perfection daily. The home cook, working with supermarket ingredients and without the help of a prep cook or a pastry chef, is hard-pressed to perform the work of many hands all by him or herself.

Still, with practice, with thought, it can be done—or done so well that only a professional food critic would notice the difference. This cookbook, written by the chefs who teach chefs, will help you learn new techniques, improve your skills, and, incidentally, make some incredible meals.

The book is divided into two sections: pantry ingredients, then parts of a meal. The pantry section offers recipes you can make ahead of time and keep on hand to enhance any dish. This includes Maui-style spice mixtures, sauces, salsas, and garnishes. The second section begins with delicious "Appetizers," perfect for party pūpūs or for starting out an elegant dinner party. The "Soups, Salads, Sandwiches, and Sides" chapter offer delectables made with local produce and market-fresh ingredients—these recipes are great for a light meal or to complement a main course. The "Entrées" chapter offers creative yet accessible main dishes worthy of a formal dinner, a casual backyard lū'au, or an island-style family meal. Finally, the "Desserts" chapter showcases spectacular sweets and creations that you can make in your own home.

If you bought this cookbook because you live here in the Islands, congratulations! Lucky you live Hawai'i! Top chefs know that fresh, high-quality ingredients make the best meals. The Maui chefs who contributed to this cookbook know their island and know their local foods. They carefully explain how to source farm-fresh produce and where to find the best local quality ingredients.

If you are taking this cookbook back to the mainland with you in hopes of recreating a few of the marvelous meals you enjoyed at the Maui Culinary Academy... you can! You may have to make a few substitutions, but with a little creativity and perhaps some store-bought ingredients, you can give your local fish, meat, and produce an Island flair.

A final word about our chefs. If you look in the Contributors section, you'll see that they're an award-winning bunch. Maui, once a culinary backwater, is now a foodie mecca, as sophisticated as New York, Paris, or Singapore. These culinary wizards don't just do local cuisine; they create world-class Maui cuisine. Now they are willing to teach you some of the tricks of the trade. Here is a *Taste of Maui* from Maui's best chefs!

FROM THE PANTRY

Farm-fresh produce and products are always a delight for home cooks, and with Maui's long-time history of agriculture—from pineapple to sugar to onions—it is easier than ever to start a stellar meal with the best ingredients. As every good chef knows, the key to easy, fast, and delicious home cooking is a well-stocked pantry. Here we offer recipes for staples you'll want to always keep on hand, such as island-style spice mixtures, tantalizing sauces, easy-to-make dressings, and tasty garnishes—items that can enhance any great Maui meal.

Oven-Dried Tomatoes

MAKES 2–3 CUPS

I grew up in South Jersey, where we grow and appreciate good tomatoes. Most people don't associate New Jersey with good produce, especially tomatoes. But think about it—it is nicknamed The Garden State! When I think of summer in South Jersey, I think of sliced tomatoes on crusty Italian bread with mayonnaise, salt, fresh ground pepper, and basil. When tomatoes are in season—and the season is very limited!—that's the time to stock up and use them in everything.

This recipe is a great, tasty, and healthy way to use garden ripe tomatoes. The intense tomato flavor marries well with the herbs, garlic and olive oil. These tomatoes aren't the usual hard, dry sun-dried tomatoes you find at the supermarket. They will only keep a week in the refrigerator—if you don't eat them all before the week is up.

I like these tomatoes chopped up and tossed with some pasta, fresh basil, olive oil, and Parmesan. They're also great on crostini with pesto and goat cheese. Throw some in the food processor with a little warm chicken stock and fresh herbs and it makes a great tomato sauce for creamy polenta. Add some to your favorite shrimp scampi recipe to give it a boost.

—*Tom Lelli*

8 vine-ripened Roma tomatoes (or other fleshy variety)	2 fresh finely chopped basil leaves
	1 teaspoon kosher salt
1 sprig finely chopped fresh rosemary	2 tablespoons extra virgin olive oil
2 sprigs finely chopped fresh thyme	Fresh ground black pepper

Preheat oven to 200 degrees.

Remove the stems from the Roma tomatoes and cut them in half lengthwise. Toss the tomatoes, herbs, salt and olive oil in a bowl and season with a few twists of fresh ground pepper.

Place a cooling rack on a cookie sheet or sheet pan and place the tomatoes skin side down on the rack. Put the pan in the oven for 3-4 hours, until tomatoes shrink by half and become slightly dry to the touch. Drying time may vary depending on your oven. Convection ovens (ovens with a fan to circulate air) work best.

Remove the tomatoes from the oven and if you are not using them right away, store them in a closed plastic container. They will keep in the refrigerator for 1 week.

Preserved Lemons

Preserved lemons are a staple in Moroccan cooking. I first made them with a student who was interested in exploring authentic Moroccan food. Now I cannot do without them. They have a wonderful lemon flavor, with more punch than the milder flavors of lemon juice or zest. I use them in any dish to which I want to add a little "zing"—dishes like stewed lentils, Poêle of Chicken (see page 144), onion relish, or gremolata.

You can add spices like peppercorns, cloves, cinnamon stick, and bay leaf for an even more authentic Moroccan flavor. The rinds are very salty, so if you add them to a dish, add less salt than you usually do.

These lemons are great in a lamb or chicken tagine (a Moroccan-style stew). I like to use them in marinades, dressings, and cooked lentils. Blend one lemon with some olive oil, lemon juice, garlic, and rosemary and you have an excellent marinade for barbecued chicken. You can rub a whole chicken with this marinade, let it sit over night, and then roast—delicious! Or try them with the Lemon Vinaigrette recipe on page 9.

—*Tom Lelli*

12–14 lemons, scrubbed	Fresh lemon juice, as needed
1 box kosher salt (you will not need the whole box)	3 wide-mouth mason jars (1-quart size), sterilized

---

Cut a thin, penny-sized slice off both ends of each lemon so that they will sit upright. Set each lemon on one of the flat ends and make a vertical cut down the center, ¾ of the way through the fruit, so that the two halves remain attached at the base. Turn each lemon upside down and make a second vertical cut at a 90-degree angle to the first, again ¾ of the way through fruit. You now have a lemon cut into quarters that are still attached.

Fill the cuts in each lemon with as much salt as they will hold. Don't worry if a lemon or two breaks in half; when you put them in the jars, you'll probably have to break a couple apart anyway.

Place the lemons in the mason jars one at a time. Press down on them so they release some of their juice. Repeat this process until it is full and the lemons are "smashed" up against each other. Top each jar with 2 tablespoons of salt—less is fine if there's not enough room for 2 tablespoons—and extra lemon juice until the lemons are covered.

(recipe continued on page 4)

With a clean, wet rag, wipe the outside of the jar, removing any excess salt, especially around the mouth where the groove touches the metal lid. Leftover salt could corrode the lid. Seal the jars with the lids and store them at room temperature for 30 days.

Every 5 days, turn the jars upside down, then set them upright again, to mix the brine and the sediments. Refrigerate after one month.

The lemons are ready to use after they have been marinated for 30 to 45 days and the rinds are tender. To use, remove and discard the pulp from the lemons and rinse the salt from the rinds. The rinds—sliced, blended, or minced—can then be used as seasoning.

As previously noted, when you use your preserved lemons, be sure to reduce the salt in your recipes, as these lemons definitely add a salty flavor.

❋ RUBS AND MARINADES ❋

Turkish Spice Rub

MAKES ENOUGH TO COAT AND SEASON 6 (8 OUNCE) PORTIONS OF MEAT

This easy-to-make and easy-to-use rub evokes the exotic, aromatic flavors of the East. It's a great rub for any meat or poultry.

—*Chris Speere*

2 tablespoons brown sugar	2 teaspoons kosher salt
4 teaspoons ground coriander	1½ teaspoons ground ginger
4 teaspoons ground cumin	1 teaspoon ground turmeric
3 teaspoons garlic powder	

Combine all ingredients and mix thoroughly. Keep in an airtight container away from direct sunlight.

TO USE THE RUB

Sprinkle the rub over the meat or seafood of your choice and rub in, making sure it sticks. Use about 1 tablespoon for each 8-ounce meat or seafood portion. Let rest for at least 20 minutes in the refrigerator before cooking.

Maui Coffee Spice Rub

At the Maui Culinary Academy, coffee does more than give you your morning jolt—it also makes an excellent spice rub that wakes up your favorite meat and fish dishes. Developed by our Research and Development students, Maui Coffee Spice Rub combines the full-bodied flavor of Maui coffee with the heat of Aleppo pepper (a coarsely ground red pepper favored in the Middle East and Central Asia and appreciated for its fragrance and flavor; it is available from online grocers).

This spice rub is perfect for grilling: just sprinkle it on chicken, pork chops or steaks. It's not just for meat; Maui Coffee Spice Rub can be used as a seafood marinade as well—try it on fish, shrimp, and scallops. This rub may well become one of your favorite seasonings.

If you'd rather not make the rub yourself, it's available for purchase at the Maui Culinary Academy and at gourmet shops throughout the islands.

—Chris Speere

1¼ cups ground coffee beans (preferably Maui-grown)	2½ tablespoons dried oregano
1¼ cups finely ground black pepper	¾ cup Aleppo pepper (can use crushed red chilli flakes as substitute)
5 tablespoons cumin powder	½ cup kosher salt

Combine all ingredients and mix thoroughly. Keep in an airtight container away from direct sunlight.

TO USE THE RUB

Sprinkle the rub over the meat or seafood of your choice and rub in, making sure it sticks. Use about 1 tablespoon for each 8-ounce meat or seafood portion. Let rest for at least 20 minutes in the refrigerator before cooking.

To make a marinade out of the rub, combine about 10 ounces of the meat of your choice with 2–3 tablespoons of rub, 1 tablespoon of olive oil, 1 clove of minced garlic, and ½ cup of red wine in a large re-sealable plastic bag. Allow to marinate for at least 2 hours or better yet, overnight, so that the meat can absorb the full flavor of the marinade. For a Mediterranean twist, make the marinade with garlic, olive oil, white wine and lemon juice. For an Asian flair, combine the rub with soy sauce, garlic, and rice wine vinegar. For a Mexican taste, combine the coffee rub with lime juice, oregano, and roasted bell peppers. Cook as desired and serve with fresh vegetables.

Adobo Marinade for Grilling

This easy, tasty, Latin-flavored marinade is great on fresh shrimp or fish, and it works equally well on grilled pork or chicken. I also use it for slow-roasted pork.

Toast the dried chillies in a heavy skillet over low heat or in the oven for a few minutes, until fragrant. This will bring out the full flavor of the chillies. Experiment with heat and taste by using different varieties of dried chillies, or by adding fresh cilantro and cumin to the marinade.

—*Tom Lelli*

1 cup toasted, seeded, and chopped chillies (use mild dried chillies such as Ancho or Pasilla)	Zest of 1 orange
	¼ cup lime juice
	¼ cup cider vinegar
3 cloves garlic	½ cup olive oil
2 shallots, peeled and chopped	1 teaspoon salt
1 tablespoon chopped oregano	1 teaspoon fresh ground pepper
1 cup orange juice	

Place chillies in a small pot of water and bring to a simmer until chillies are rehydrated and soft. Drain and cool chillies.

Place chillies in a blender or food processor with all the ingredients except the olive oil. Process until it becomes a smooth paste. Slowly add the oil until the marinade is thoroughly mixed.

Brush marinade on shrimp or fish ¼ hour before grilling. Brush on chicken or meat 2-4 hours before grilling or let marinate overnight. Season with salt and pepper before cooking.

Fish Stock

Rather than discarding the bones and trimmings from freshly butchered fish, you can put them to good use for fish stock. We make fish stock every time we butcher fresh fish; you can too. Instead of discarding the fish bones and trimmings, follow the recipe for a fool-proof stock with a clean fresh flavor. It makes a terrific base for any seafood soup or sauce—try it with the Lavender Infused Island Seafood Chowder on page 49.

The stock is made with a mixture of chopped onions, leeks, and celery. This combination is known as white mirepoix.

—Dean Louie

2 pounds fish trimmings and bones, rinsed (do not use the stomach, blood line, or gills)	1 gallon cold water
	2 bay leaves
	1 tablespoon fresh or dried thyme
1 pound of roughly chopped onions, leeks, and celery (approximately ⅓ pound of each vegetable)	1 tablespoon cracked black peppercorns (see tip on page 174)

In a large stockpot, cover the trimmings and mirepoix with cold water and bring to a boil. Immediately turn down the heat to a slight, slow simmer. Do not let the stock boil again. Skim the foam from the surface of the stock. Add the peppercorns and bay leaf.

Simmer for 30 minutes only, carefully skimming foam from the surface every 15 minutes.

Carefully strain the stock and discard the bones. Keep the stock warm or quickly chill for later use.

Vinaigrettes will last three to five days if kept in a tightly covered container and refrigerated. Don't forget to shake the vinaigrette well before using.

Carrot Vinaigrette

MAKES 4 SERVINGS

Maui Culinary Academy graduate Malia Lamadora created this great-tasting and colorful vinaigrette. I was so impressed by this dressing that I introduced it to our student-run Leis Family Class Act Restaurant.

For an Asian flavor, add a small piece of ginger when juicing the carrots. This vinaigrette is great served over grilled vegetables.

—*Tom Lelli*

1 cup sliced carrot (cut 1-inch thick)	2 tablespoons Dijon mustard
2 tablespoons rice wine vinegar	1 teaspoon honey
⅓ cup olive oil	Salt and white pepper

Juice the carrot slices in a juicer. Simmer the carrot juice in a saucepot over medium-high heat until it is reduced by ⅔. Pour the juice into a bowl and mix with the rice wine vinegar, olive oil, and Dijon mustard until emulsified. Add the honey to the mixture and season with salt and white pepper.

Mango Vinaigrette

MAKES 4 CUPS

This vinaigrette provides a sweet, creamy counterpart to salad greens, and it can also be used as a dipping sauce for seafood. I created it to go with the Black Pepper Prawns with Mixed Greens on page 96.

—*Dean Louie*

2 ripe mangoes, peeled and seeded	2 cups olive oil
2 shallots, peeled and chopped	¼ to ½ teaspoon sugar, depending on
1 tablespoon Dijon mustard	your taste
1 cup rice wine vinegar	Salt and white pepper to taste

Prepare the vinaigrette by slowly adding oil while puréeing the rest of the ingredients in a food processor. You can also use an immersion blender. Season to taste and chill before serving.

Lemon Vinaigrette

There's no reason to use bottled vinaigrette when the real thing is so easy to make. This particular recipe is very versatile. You can substitute your favorite light vinegar for the white balsamic vinegar. Try a little walnut oil or use herbs such as tarragon or basil. Of course, vinaigrette is not just for salad anymore—try it on your favorite fish or fresh steamed vegetables.

—Tom Lelli

¼ cup lemon juice, fresh	1 sprig fresh thyme, leaves only
1 teaspoon preserved lemon, rinsed (see Preserved Lemon recipe page 3); you can also substitute lemon zest for the preserved lemon	2 tablespoons white balsamic vinegar
	1 teaspoon Dijon mustard
	1 cup extra virgin olive oil
1 teaspoon shallot, minced	Salt and fresh ground pepper

In a small bowl, whisk together all ingredients except the oil. Slowly whisk in the oil to form an emulsion, in which the oil forms such tiny droplets that it appears to have dissolved in the vinegar. Season with salt and pepper to taste.

Tomato Vinaigrette

Fresh, flavorful tomatoes are a key component to the success in this recipe. Tomato vinaigrette can be used as a salsa, dipping sauce, or on pasta. It has Italian flavor overtones that go well with most dishes.

Try this vinaigrette with the Pan-Seared Shrimp and Pancetta-Wrapped Scallop Skewers on page 42.

—Chris Speere

10 Roma tomatoes, seeded and finely diced	2 cloves garlic, peeled and minced
1 cup olive oil	2 tablespoons balsamic vinegar
¼ cup finely chopped red onion	2 tablespoons lemon juice
¼ cup finely chopped flat leaf parsley	1 teaspoon Dijon mustard
	Salt and pepper to taste

Put all the ingredients for the vinaigrette into a large mixing bowl. Toss gently. Set aside at room temperature for 2 minutes to allow the flavors to blend.

Honey-Citrus Dressing

This dressing combines tangy orange and honey flavors, and also works well with any salad greens. Also try it on grilled white fish such as 'ōpakapaka or moi. I created it to go with the Macadamia Nut, Watercress, and Belgian Endive Citrus Salad on page 54.

—*Chris Speere*

¾ cup orange juice
¼ cup white wine vinegar
¼ cup olive oil
3 tablespoons honey
1 tablespoon finely chopped shallots

1 tablespoon Dijon mustard
½ teaspoon salt
½ teaspoon ground black pepper
3 tablespoons chopped flat leaf
  parsley

Mix all ingredients thoroughly. Set the dressing aside for at least 10 minutes so that the flavors can combine. If there is time, a 1 hour rest is best.

Soy-Ginger Vinaigrette

Add simple Asian-style flavor to vegetables with this easy vinaigrette. You can also use it as a dipping sauce for spring rolls or toss with rice noodles. I created it to go with the Lotus and Asparagus Salad on page 52.

—*Kyle Kawakami*

½ cup canola oil
3 tablespoons sesame oil
3 tablespoons rice wine vinegar

3 tablespoons sugar
3 tablespoons soy sauce
2 tablespoons finely grated ginger

Place all the ingredients in a one-quart bowl and whisk together vigorously for 1 minute. Refrigerate for at least 1 hour to let flavors combine.

Warm Macadamia Nut Oil and Ginger Vinaigrette

MAKES ½ CUP

Macadamia nut oil adds a subtle, nutty flavor to this vinaigrette, while the ginger and soy sauce add an Asian flair. Try the warm vinaigrette with mesclun greens, grilled fish, or pair it with the Macadamia Nut Prawn Tempura on page 95.

—*Darryl Dela Cruz*

4 tablespoons macadamia nut oil	1 teaspoon minced garlic
1 teaspoon finely chopped ginger	2 tablespoons soy sauce
1 teaspoon finely chopped shallot	1 teaspoon sugar
1 teaspoon Thai chilli sauce	2 tablespoons rice vinegar

In a small saucepot, heat 2 tablespoons of the macadamia nut oil, then add the ginger and shallots. Cook on medium-low heat until the spices are fragrant, or about 5 minutes. Add the chilli sauce, garlic, soy sauce, and sugar; simmer for 1 minute. Add the rest of the macadamia nut oil and the rice vinegar.

Using a hand held blender, process the vinaigrette until well emulsified. (If you do not have an immersion blender, whisk the vinaigrette vigorously.) Keep warm until ready to serve.

Tropical Maui Salsa

MAKES APPROXIMATELY 5 CUPS

This is one of the first recipes we created at the Maui Prince Hotel back in 1986. For me, it evokes the excitement of the time when Hawai'i Regional Cuisine was emerging.

This salsa is a good accompaniment to poultry or fish. The cilantro and chilli sauce provide a complementary spark to the sweet, mellow fruit flavors.

—Chris Speere

1 cup finely diced mango
1 cup finely diced papaya
½ cup finely diced Maui Gold pineapple
1 cup finely diced fresh lychee fruit
½ cup finely chopped Maui onion
¼ cup finely diced red bell pepper
¼ cup finely diced green bell pepper
½ cup finely diced fresh water chestnuts

½ cup minced fresh cilantro leaves
⅛ cup chopped fresh mint

DRESSING
2 tablespoons fresh lime juice (you can use more or less to your taste)
2 tablespoons sweet Thai chilli sauce
½ tablespoon rice vinegar (or to taste)

Combine the ingredients for the dressing. Set aside.

Lightly mix all the salsa ingredients together in a large non-reactive (stainless steel or glass) bowl. Add the dressing. Taste the salsa, then adjust flavors to taste.

This salsa may be served immediately, or stored covered, in the refrigerator for 2–3 days. Bring chilled salsa to room temperature before serving.

Maui Culinary Academy's Pineapple Ginger Salsa

MAKES 2 CUPS

This dish was created as a new and innovative way to utilize the Roasted Pineapple Jam produced by our Research and Development students at the Maui Culinary Academy. The salsa has a wonderfully sweet flavor and can be used to spark a multitude of dishes, from fish tacos to chicken salads. Try serving it with fresh corn tortilla chips as a delicious alternative to store-bought salsa.

The Maui Roasted Pineapple Jam is available for purchase at the Maui Culinary Academy and at gourmet shops throughout the islands.

—*Kyle Kawakami*

1 jar (10 ounce size) Maui Culinary Academy Roasted Pineapple Jam	¼ cup chopped cilantro
½ cup finely diced red onion (you can substitute Maui onion)	1 tablespoon minced ginger
2 tomatoes, finely diced	Juice of one lemon
1 small fresh jalapeño pepper, seeded and minced	Salt and pepper

Place all salsa ingredients into a mixing bowl. Combine gently until well mixed. Taste and adjust seasoning if necessary. Refrigerate until ready to serve.

Tomato Salsa Fresca

MAKES 1 CUP

This versatile salsa is made with fresh tomatoes—use the freshest you can find for the best flavor. The salsa goes well with practically everything, such as pastas, seafood, chicken, or even vegetables. I created this recipe to go with the Grilled Vegetable Crêpes with Goat Cheese on page 86.

—*Tom Lelli*

2 large ripe tomatoes, chopped into ½-inch dice	2 tablespoons ounce olive oil
½ red onion, finely chopped	1 teaspoon red wine vinegar
1 sprig fresh basil, chopped	Salt and fresh ground pepper

Mix all ingredients together in a bowl until they are well combined. Season with salt and pepper.

Maui Arugula & Macadamia Nut Pesto

MAKES 1 CUP

This recipe was created to help local Maui farmers find new uses for the excellent and abundant Maui arugula. Pesto is traditionally made from sweet Italian basil. I substituted our peppery local arugula for the basil, giving a flavorful twist to the traditional recipe.

Mix with fresh cooked pasta; use as a spread on grilled breads or as a marinade on fish or chicken (see page 142). Add a few spoonfuls to your favorite vinaigrette recipe to give a fresh and nutty accent to your salads. This pesto can be stored as long as 2 weeks in the refrigerator.

—Chris Speere

1 cup arugula	3 cloves garlic
1 cup Italian parsley	¼ cup olive oil
¼ cup lemon juice	½ cup freshly grated Parmesan
½ cup toasted and chopped macadamia nuts (see page 174 for tips)	cheese
	Salt and black pepper

Blanch the arugula in salted boiling water for approximately 1 minute. Drain it and quickly plunge it into an ice bath; this stops the cooking process. Drain well, then squeeze out any remaining water.

Roughly chop the arugula, then pulse for 2 minutes in a food processor with the parsley, lemon juice, and a pinch of salt. Add the toasted macadamia nuts and garlic; pulse for another minute or so. The pesto should form a mealy paste. Add the olive oil in a slow stream while puréeing the mixture; continue puréeing until the paste is smooth. Fold in the grated Parmesan cheese and season to taste with salt and pepper.

Green Onion Pesto

MAKES 1 CUP

This island-style pesto features green onions, parsley, and macadamia nuts—a winning combination for the Kālua Pork Sandwich on page 69. You can also use the pesto as a spread for other meat or vegetable sandwiches, or try it with pasta for a nice side dish.

—Darryl Dela Cruz

½ cup roughly chopped green onions	½ cup olive oil
¼ cup roughly chopped parsley	2 tablespoons grated asiago or
¼ cup roughly chopped macadamia nuts	Parmesan cheese

Place the scallions, parsley, and macadamia nuts in the bowl of a food processor. While the processor is running, slowly add the oil and then the cheese. Process until smooth. Season with salt and pepper to taste.

Olive Relish

MAKES 2 CUPS

This relish is good to have in your pūpū repertoire—it works well on crackers or toasted French or Italian bread, and is also good in panini sandwiches. I like to serve it with the elegant 'Ahi Carpaccio recipe on page 40.

—Tom Lelli

2 tablespoons extra virgin olive oil	½ teaspoon sugar
½ cup finely diced red onion	½ cup finely chopped Greek olives
1 medium red bell pepper, finely diced	½ cup finely chopped green olives
1 clove garlic, minced	1 sprig fresh basil, chopped
2 tablespoons sherry vinegar	Salt and freshly ground pepper to taste

Heat the olive oil in a non-stick sauté pan over low heat. Sauté the onion, bell pepper and garlic in the olive oil for approximately 3 minutes or until soft. Add the sherry vinegar and sugar, increase the heat to medium, and cook gently until most of the liquid is gone, which should take about 5 minutes. Remove the mixture from the heat and let it cool.

In a stainless steel bowl, mix the remaining relish ingredients with the onion-pepper mixture, season to taste, and refrigerate.

Maui Corn Relish

You can't beat fresh corn, especially when grown locally. The Uradomo family of upcountry Kula, here on Maui, grows some of the best corn in Hawai'i. The kernels are full, firm, and sweet. They add the perfect touch of sweetness to this dish.

Serve the relish with your favorite fish dish, or try it with the Pan-Seared 'Ōpakapaka on page 110.

—*Chris Speere*

---

3 ears Maui corn, kernels only (or any fresh, local corn from your area)
2 tablespoons canola oil
1 teaspoon salt
½ teaspoon pepper
2 cups diced fresh shiitake mushrooms

½ cup finely diced daikon
1 large tomato, finely diced
½ cup chopped green onion
2 tablespoons rice wine vinegar
1 tablespoon sugar

Heat the canola oil in a large sauté pan and add the corn kernels. Cook them on high heat for 1 minute. Season the corn with salt and pepper and set aside in a small mixing bowl. Leave the pan on the stove.

Now add the shiitake mushrooms, daikon, tomatoes, and green onions the to heated sauté pan and cook over medium heat for 3 minutes. Put the cooked corn kernels back into the pan. Quickly mix the vegetables, remove the pan from the heat, and add the rice vinegar and sugar. Mix well and correct the seasoning, if necessary, with salt and pepper.

The relish can be stored covered, in the refrigerator, for up to one week.

Ginger Beurre Blanc Sauce

MAKES 1 CUP

Beurre blanc means "white butter" in French. It begins with a reduction of vinegar or white wine and chopped shallots. (To reduce means to cook down, to reduce the volume and intensify the flavor.) The reduction is taken off the heat and cold butter is added. The butter melts, making a rich sauce.

This beurre blanc has an additional ginger flavor. The sauce goes well with any white fish, salmon, or even lobster. Try it with the Pan-Seared 'Ōpakapaka on page 110.

—*Chris Speere*

2 tablespoons chopped ginger	1 cup cream
2 tablespoons chopped shallots	8 tablespoons (1 stick) butter, cold, cut
1 teaspoon black peppercorns	into small cubes
1 cup dry white wine	

In a medium-size saucepot, over medium heat, simmer the ginger, shallots, peppercorns and white wine for approximately 5 minutes, or until the liquid is reduced to ⅓ of its former volume. Add the cream and reduce again by ⅔.

Remove the saucepot from the heat and slowly whisk in the cold cubed butter until the butter is thoroughly incorporated, or about 2 minutes. Strain the sauce into a small pot and keep it warm on the top of the stove.

Basil Cream Sauce

MAKES 1 CUP

I created this sauce to go with the Moloka'i Sweet Potato Shrimp Cakes on page 94, but it also goes well with any other pan-fried cakes such as crab cakes, taro cakes, and salmon cakes.

—*Chris Speere*

1 cup heavy cream	2 tablespoons chopped fresh basil
1 clove garlic, roasted and chopped	Pinch of nutmeg
¼ cup grated Parmesan cheese	Salt and pepper to taste
2 tablespoons salted butter, softened	

In a saucepan over medium heat, bring the cream to a boil. Reduce the heat to low. Add the garlic, stir in the Parmesan cheese, and slowly whisk in the softened butter. Stir in the basil and nutmeg and blend until smooth. Season to taste.

Thai Peanut Curry Sauce

MAKES 3 CUPS

We are so fortunate here in Hawai'i to enjoy a myriad of exceptional cuisines, Thai cuisine among them. Thai chefs and cooks have shared their expertise and recipes with all of us here in the Islands, expanding our daily repertoire and restaurant menus in delightful ways.

This sauce complements almost any grilled food item. Serve with skewered beef, chicken, tofu or shrimp to transform them into satay. This sauce is especially good as a dipping sauce for Thai summer or spring rolls.

—Chris Speere

2 cups coconut milk	¼ cup red curry paste
½ cup creamy peanut butter	¼ cup minced shallots
¼ cup brown sugar	2 tablespoons minced garlic
¼ cup soy sauce	2 tablespoons finely chopped
1 tablespoon rice vinegar	lemongrass (bottom stalk only)
2 kaffir lime leaves	2 tablespoons fish sauce
¼ cup julienned Thai basil	1 cup finely chopped cilantro

Combine all ingredients in a non-reactive saucepan. Use stainless steel, glass, or Teflon, not aluminum. Over medium-high heat, bring ingredients to a simmer. Reduce the heat to medium-low and cook slowly until sauce starts to thicken and coats the back of a serving spoon; this will take approximately 10–15 minutes. Stir sauce periodically to check the consistency. Let cool. Remove and discard the lime leaves before serving.

Serve this sauce hot over skewered grilled meats and seafood. It can be stored, refrigerated, for up to one week.

Sweet Wasabi Sauce

This dipping sauce was a winner of the 2005 Gohan (rice) in New York recipe contest sponsored by Japan's Department of Agriculture. The contest promoted Japanese heirloom rice. This is a delicious and interesting alternative to the more common wasabi/soy sauce combination. Try this sauce with the Crispy Lobster Cone Sushi on page 98.

—*Chris Speere*

6 tablespoons mayonnaise	2 teaspoons honey
2 tablespoons red Tobiko caviar	1 tablespoon orange juice
2 teaspoons Dijon mustard	1 teaspoon orange zest
2 teaspoons wasabi paste	½ teaspoon soy sauce

Mix all ingredients thoroughly in a bowl. Refrigerate until ready to serve.

The sauce can be kept in the refrigerator for up to 2-3 days in a tightly covered container.

Sweet Soy Syrup

I created this sweet sauce as a contrast to the Ginger Beurre Blanc Sauce (see page 17). Both sauces pair well with the Pan-Seared 'Ōpakapaka on page 110. You can also use this sweet syrup on its own. Try it with other fish dishes or for something different, try it with sushi.

—*Chris Speere*

½ cup mirin	1 teaspoon sugar
¼ cup soy sauce	3 tablespoons sake

Combine all the ingredients in a small saucepot and bring to a boil over high heat. Reduce heat to low and simmer until the sauce thickens to a syrup. The syrup shouldn't be too thick. This may take 2–3 minutes. Let the syrup cool to room temperature before serving.

Caper Lemon Relish Sauce

MAKES 1¼ CUPS

This sauce goes perfectly with the Island-Style Fish and Chips on page 118, but you can use it as a tasty substitute for tartar sauce. The capers and pickle relish add a great tang to the creaminess of the mayonnaise. Try the sauce with other batter-fried seafood or even on fish, lobster, or crab sandwiches.

—*Darryl Dela Cruz*

¾ cup mayonnaise	2 tablespoons lemon juice
⅓ cup pickle relish	Salt and pepper to taste
3 tablespoons drained and chopped capers	

Combine all the ingredients in a small mixing bowl and mix well. Refrigerate until ready to use.

Wasabi Aioli

MAKES ¼ CUP

This simple aioli uses prepared mayonnaise, which saves time from making your own. It goes well with sushi and sashimi, including the Peppered 'Ahi Sashimi on page 27.

—*Dean Louie*

1 tablespoon wasabi paste	½ teaspoon minced garlic
¼ cup mayonnaise	Juice of one lemon

Mix all of the ingredients together until well-combined. Refrigerate until ready to use.

Roasted Garlic Aioli

Aioli is a sauce made from garlic and olive oil, and sometimes an egg to help emulsify the two ingredients. This aioli variation uses roasted garlic, which is mellower than raw garlic, yet still gives a nice garlicky flavor.

This sauce is great for garlic lovers. Try it with French fries, or on seafood or shellfish. It goes wonderfully with the elegant 'Ahi Carpaccio appetizer on page 40.

—*Tom Lelli*

1 head fresh garlic	Zest of 1 lemon
1 egg	½ cup extra virgin olive oil
1 egg yolk	½ cup canola or other neutral oil
2 tablespoons fresh lemon juice	Salt and white pepper to taste

TO PREPARE THE ROASTED GARLIC

Preheat the oven to 350 degrees. Rub the head of garlic with a little olive oil, wrap it in a piece of foil, and place the garlic in the oven for some 45 minutes or until it becomes soft and fragrant. Remove the garlic from the oven and let it to cool.

When the garlic is cool, cut off the top end of the head and gently squeeze out the roasted garlic. It should be soft.

TO PREPARE THE AIOLI

Place 1 tablespoon of the roasted garlic in the bowl of a food processor with the egg, egg yolk, lemon juice, and lemon zest. With the machine running, very slowly add all the oil, first a few drops at a time, then in a thin, steady stream. The sauce will emulsify and thicken. Remove the aioli from the processor bowl and season it with salt and white pepper to taste.

Raspberry Coulis

MAKES 1½ CUPS

This easy-to-make dessert sauce goes perfectly with chocolate cake, cheese cake, or even our favorite Roselani Tropics Hawaiian Vanilla Bean ice cream. The raspberries add a bright and not too tart flavor, perfect for livening up any sweet dish. Try the coulis with the Pineapple Fritters on page 164.

—Chris Speere

12 oz. frozen raspberries, thawed and drained or 1 lb. fresh raspberries ¼ to ⅓ cup sugar	1 tablespoon fresh lemon juice, or to taste

Combine the raspberries, ¼ cup sugar, and lemon juice in a food processor or blender. Puree until well blended. Taste mixture and add more sugar if you want it sweeter.

Press the mixture through a fine sieve or mesh strainer to remove the seeds. Discard the solids. Refrigerate the strained puree until ready to use.

You can store the coulis in the refrigerator for up to 5 days in a tightly covered container.

Mango Purée

MAKES 1½ CUPS

Mangoes are abundant during most of the year on Maui. This sweet, ubiquitous fruit can be used simply diced in fruit salsas, or puréed in no-cook sauces like this. This dessert sauce is very simple and goes wonderfully with any sweet treat such as angel food cake, Key lime pie, or of course, our favorite Roselani Tropics Hawaiian Vanilla Bean ice cream. You'll also love it with the Pineapple Fritters on page 164.

—Chris Speere

3 mangoes, peeled, pitted, and diced 2-3 tablespoons sugar	1 tablespoon fresh lemon juice, or to taste

Combine the mangoes, 2 tablespoons sugar, and lemon juice in a food processor or blender. Purée until smooth. Taste mixture and add more sugar if you want it sweeter. Refrigerate the purée until ready to use.

You can store the purée in the refrigerator for up to 5 days in a tightly covered container.

Avocado Butter

MAKES 1 CUP

Fresh avocado is enhanced with creamy butter to create this delicious topping. Serve a dollop or two of the flavored butter on top of freshly-cooked fish such as 'ōpakapaka, onaga, moi, or opah. Or try it with the Pan-Seared Mahimahi entrée on page 122.

—Bob Cambra

8 tablespoons (1 stick) butter, softened	1 tablespoon chopped garlic
¼ cup diced red onion	Juice of one lime
¼ cup minced green onion	1 avocado, diced

Mix the butter in a bowl until creamy. Add the red onion, green onion, garlic, and lime juice; mix well. Fold in the avocado. Season to taste with salt and pepper. Hold at room temperature if the dish is to be served immediately. Otherwise, refrigerate until 30 minutes before you are ready to serve.

❋ **GARNISHES** ❋

Won Ton Pi Chips

MAKES 24 CHIPS

We use quite a few of these chips every day. Made fresh, they're oh-so-'ono. You can make them ahead of time; they'll lose a little of the freshness, but they'll still be better than commercial chips.

Try these chips with 'Ahi Poke (page 26), or Roasted Maui Gold Pineapple Thai Ceviche (page 28), or Maui Coffee Spice Rub Pulled Pork (page 30). They're also a tasty accent to many other dishes.

—Ben Marquez

12 won ton wrappers
2 cups of cooking oil (vegetable, canola, corn, or peanut oil)

Cut each won ton pi wrapper in half diagonally. Fry in 350 degree oil until golden brown and crispy, or about 2–3 minutes per side. Drain on paper towels.

These won ton chips can be made ahead of time and kept in air-tight plastic bags for up to one week.

Crème Fraîche

Crème fraîche is a wonderful staple ingredient to have on hand in your refrigerator. It adds lush, creamy texture and a bit of tartness to your favorite dishes. Use crème fraîche in place of sour cream and you'll be pleased with the results. As is often the case, this homemade version of crème fraîche is far superior to any store-bought product. Use it on baked potatoes, on top of crêpes or pancakes, or folded into mashed potatoes.

—*Chris Speere*

2 cups heavy cream	**½ cup sour cream**
½ cup buttermilk	**¼ teaspoon salt**

Combine all ingredients in a clean, non-reactive (stainless steel or glass) saucepan. Blend the ingredients thoroughly and heat to a temperature of 100 degrees. Transfer the mixture to a clean stainless steel bowl, cover with plastic wrap, and set into a gas oven heated only by the pilot light. If you have an electric oven, set the oven to 70 or 75 degrees. If your house isn't too cold, room temperature may also suffice.

Leave the crème to set for 12 hours. Remove bowl from oven and place in refrigerator for 24 hours. Carefully remove the thickened top or "crème fraîche." Discard any liquid left at the bottom. Place crème fraîche in a covered container in the refrigerator until ready to use. It will keep in the refrigerator for up to 3 weeks.

APPETIZERS

Get the meal started with these mouthwatering recipes, which set the stage for a complete Maui-style menu. Take advantage of the sea's fresh bounty by starting off with stellar poke, savory sashimi, or satisfying ceviche. Or try our suggestions for party-style hors d'oeuvres and bite-sized treats, full of big, fresh flavors that will keep your family and guests asking for seconds.

'Ahi Poke

Once, it was a daring innovation to add oyster sauce to poke; now oyster sauce is considered an everyday favorite. This widely available condiment adds a familiar Asian touch to the raw tuna and freshly toasted sesame seeds add texture and flavor to the poke. Be careful, though, with this salty sauce—a little goes a long way!

—*Dean Louie*

---

2 pounds fresh 'ahi block, cut into
   1-inch cubes
3 tablespoons oyster sauce
2 tablespoons finely diced Maui onion
1 teaspoon sugar
1 teaspoon sesame oil
1 teaspoon soy sauce
1 teaspoon red chilli flakes or minced
   fresh Hawaiian chilli pepper

Juice of 1 lemon
2 tablespoons thinly sliced green
   onions
1 tablespoon white sesame seeds,
   toasted (see page 174 for tips)
Sesame Cucumber Salad (recipe on
   page 60)
Won ton pi chips (recipe on page 23)

Combine the oyster sauce, Maui onion, sugar, sesame oil, soy sauce, chilli, and lemon juice and mix well. Chill. Put the 'ahi in a mixing bowl and gently coat it with some of the marinade. Taste an 'ahi cube. Is there enough marinade? Add the marinade a little at a time until the poke is seasoned to taste. Be careful not to add too much, as the marinade is salty.

For an elegant arrangement, lay out 6–10 salad plates. Drain the cucumber salad and place about 4 tablespoons of salad at the center of each plate. Put approximately 3 tablespoons of poke on top of each salad. Garnish with won ton chips, green onion, and sesame seeds.

To serve this dish family-style, mound the poke in the center of a large platter. Garnish generously with thinly sliced green onions and sesame seeds. Drain the cucumber salad and arrange it around the circumference of the poke. Serve the poke with a bowl of won ton pi chips and let everyone dig in!

Peppered 'Ahi Sashimi

This sashimi dish tickles your palate with a medley of spicy, sweet, and salty tastes, flavors which highlight the rich smoothness of 'ahi, the "Beef of the Sea." The recipe is low in fat and cholesterol, but it doesn't sacrifice rich taste for health. You will want to cook the 'ahi quickly, just enough to caramelize the peppery crust. Make sure there is plenty of cross-ventilation in the kitchen when you are searing the fish.

—*Dean Louie*

---

2 fresh 'ahi blocks, sashimi grade, 2 x 2 x 6-inch, approximately 1½ pounds total
1 tablespoon cracked black peppercorns (see tip on page 174)
1 tablespoon sugar (optional)

1 teaspoon kosher salt
1 teaspoon crushed red chilli flakes
Neutral oil, like canola, for searing
Wasabi Aioli (see page 20)
2 tablespoons grated fresh daikon
2 tablespoons finely sliced green onion

TO PREPARE THE 'AHI

Mix the pepper, sugar, salt, and chilli flakes and distribute the mixture evenly on a flat surface; a large flat dinner plate works well.

Heat a medium-size non-stick sauté pan over high heat. When the pan is very hot, add a little oil to lightly cover the bottom. Roll the 'ahi blocks in the spice mixture to coat all sides. Sear the blocks on all four sides, for about 20 seconds per side, until the 'ahi is nicely browned and caramelized on the outside but still medium-rare in the middle. Put the 'ahi into the refrigerator, uncovered, so that it cools quickly and does not continue cooking.

TO SERVE

Cut the cooled 'ahi into thin slices, about ½ inch thick, and divide into 6 equal servings. Serve with wasabi aioli and/or soy sauce for dipping. Garnish with daikon and green onion.

Roasted Maui Gold Pineapple Thai Ceviche

Ceviche was invented in Latin America but this simple, tasty fish dish is now popular the world over. Raw fish is marinated in citrus juice which "cooks" it without heat. Roasted Maui Gold pineapple adds a unique smoky sweetness to this flavorful and refreshing island-style Thai ceviche.

Chef Becky Speere, who just happens to be my wife, is the inspiration for this wonderful ceviche. Crisp fresh herbs—Thai basil, cilantro, and mint—are musts for this recipe. If you love 'ahi, you can substitute it for the snapper.

—Chris Speere

2 cups Maui Gold pineapple, cut into ¼-inch cubes	½ cup finely chopped green onion
1½ pounds fresh Island snapper	¼ cup finely chopped fresh Thai basil leaves
¾ cup fresh-squeezed lime juice	3 teaspoons Sriracha hot chilli sauce or 2 teaspoons minced Thai dragon pepper
1 cup julienned Maui onion, 1 ½ -inch lengths	1 cup coconut milk
1 cup peeled, seeded, julienned cucumber	2 tablespoons fish sauce
½ cup finely chopped fresh mint leaves	1 teaspoon Maui Brand Natural White Cane sugar
⅓ cup finely chopped fresh cilantro	

Preheat oven to 350 degrees.

Using a very sharp knife, cut off the crown of the pineapple. Cut the fruit in half and then into quarters. Trim off the center core. Cut the fruit from the shell and cut each spear into ¼-inch cubes. Place the diced fruit onto a flat baking pan and roast in a 350 degree oven for 45 minutes or until the fruit turns golden brown. Remove the pineapple from the oven and let it set at room temperature until cool.

Cut the fish into ¼-inch cubes and place into a large glass bowl. Add fresh lime juice and marinate the fish in the refrigerator for 15 minutes. Do not drain.

TO SERVE

Remove the bowl from refrigerator and add the cooled roasted pineapple. Add the remaining ingredients: onion, cucumber, mint, cilantro, green onion, basil, hot sauce (or peppers), coconut milk, fish sauce, and sugar. Mix thoroughly.

Serve ice cold on crispy romaine lettuce leaves, with won ton pi chips (see page 23), or in chilled martini glasses.

Maui Coffee Spice Rub Pulled Pork on Won Ton Pi Chips

This dish features pork cooked local-style, in a wrapping of ti leaves. The aromatic flavors of coffee, smoke, and Turkish Aleppo pepper in our own Maui Culinary Academy Coffee Spice Rub add richness to the pulled pork. These intense flavors are balanced by the sweetness of the Maui Roasted Pineapple Jam and the earthiness of the Makawao oyster mushroom topping. Surfing Goat Dairy's Mandalay Cheese adds a creamy yet slightly spicy finish to each exciting bite.

This is the perfect appetizer for all occasions! A well-chilled Chardonnay or Sauvignon Blanc is the perfect complement to this dish.

The Maui Roasted Pineapple Jam is available for purchase at the Maui Culinary Academy and at gourmet shops throughout the islands. As a substitute, use your favorite fruit jam.

—Chris Speere

---

6 pounds pork shoulder or pork butt
2 tablespoons Maui Coffee Spice Rub (see page 5)
½ teaspoon liquid smoke
½ cup water
4 large ti leaves
1 jar Maui Roasted Pineapple Jam (9-ounce size)
½ cup Surfing Goat dairy Mandalay Goat Cheese (or soft cream cheese or crème fraîche—see recipe on page 24; add a touch of curry powder for flavor)

Won ton pi chips (see recipe on page 23)

OVEN-ROASTED MAKAWAO OYSTER MUSHROOMS

2 cups oyster mushrooms (Makawao mushrooms if available)
¼ cup olive oil
1 tablespoon chopped garlic
1 teaspoon salt
2 teaspoons black pepper
¼ cup chopped flat parsley

TO PREPARE THE PORK

Preheat the oven to 350 degrees. Line the bottom of a small roasting pan with half of the ti leaves. Place the pork on top of the leaves and rub it generously with Maui Coffee Spice Rub. Sprinkle the liquid smoke over the pork. Add the water to roasting pan and cover the pork with the remaining ti leaves. Tightly seal the roasting pan with aluminum foil and place in the preheated oven. Roast for 3 hours, or until the pork pulls apart easily when tugged with a fork.

Remove the pork from the oven and let it sit at room temperature for 1 hour. Shred the pork into small pieces and mix well with the pan juices. Set aside.

TO PREPARE THE MUSHROOMS

Break the oyster mushroom clusters into individual segments. They break apart very easily. Lightly toss the mushrooms with the olive oil, garlic, salt, and pepper. Put the mushrooms in a pan and roast at 350 degrees for 15 minutes or until golden brown. Remove them from the oven and mix in the chopped parsley. Set aside, keeping them at room temperature.

TO SERVE

Mix together the mushrooms and the pork. Place the won ton pi chips on large platter. Top each chip with approximately 1 tablespoon of the pork and mushroom mixture. Add ½ teaspoon of Maui Roasted Pineapple Jam. Finish each crisp with a small dollop of goat cheese. Serve immediately.

Island Shrimp Cocktail with Papaya-Tomato Salsa

SERVES 4

Shrimp cocktail is an old favorite, served millions of times in thousands of restaurants around the world. I asked myself, "How can I make this local? How can I take it to the next level?" Here's the answer!

I usually use 21/25 shrimp. That means that there are 21 to 25 pieces per pound. I would suggest that you use shrimp at least this large; larger is fine too. The larger the shrimp, the smaller the number.

—*Lyndon Honda*

¼ cup peanut oil
20 pieces of 21/25 shrimp
¼ cup sweet Thai chilli sauce
¼ cup plum sauce
1 tablespoon finely chopped cilantro
1 teaspoon sesame seeds, toasted
  (optional; see page 174 for tips)
1 tablespoon thinly sliced green onion
4 sprigs cilantro
8 plantain chips (slice 1 plantain
  lengthwise and deep fry until
  golden brown)

PAPAYA-TOMATO SALSA
1 cup finely diced ripe papaya
1 cup finely diced red onion
1 cup finely diced vine-ripened
  tomato
½ jalapeño pepper, minced
1 tablespoon finely chopped cilantro
1 teaspoon lime juice
Salt to taste

(recipe continued on page 33)

TO PREPARE THE SALSA

Combine all ingredients in a mixing bowl and mix well. Hold at room temperature until time to serve.

TO PREPARE THE SHRIMP

In a large sauté pan over medium heat, heat the peanut oil until it just begins to smoke, about 1 minute. Add the shrimp and partially cook them. This takes approximately 1 minute. The shrimp will be partially translucent and just beginning to turn pink. Be careful not to overcook them.

Add the sweet Thai chilli sauce, plum sauce, and cilantro. Continue cooking until the shrimp are almost done, another 2 minutes or so. The shrimp are sufficiently cooked when they have turned completely pink. Remove the shrimp from the pan; they will continue to cook as they cool. Let them cool for a few minutes, then refrigerate until time to serve.

Gently cook the liquid remaining in the pan over medium heat until it is reduced to a syrup, about 2–3 minutes. Cool the reduction to room temperature and then refrigerate until it is time to serve the dish.

TO SERVE

Divide the papaya-tomato salsa equally among 4 large martini glasses. Put the sautéed shrimp into a large bowl, drizzle them with the reduced cooking juices, and mix until the shrimp are well-coated. Place 5 seasoned shrimp on the salsa in each glass. Garnish with green onions, a cilantro sprig, plantain chips, and if desired, sesame seeds.

Pink Salmon Cakes

This recipe was created for a special video series produced by Maui Culinary Academy in conjunction with Maui Economic Opportunity. They asked our Academy's chefs to create healthy and nutritious recipes using products from the Maui Food Bank.

These salmon cakes are easy to make and inexpensive. Not only that, they are delicious. Serve them with a green salad or pair them with the Maui Corn Chowder on page 48.

—Dean Louie

1 can (10-ounce size) pink salmon	2 tablespoons finely diced canned beets
½ cup mayonnaise	1 teaspoon chopped fresh cilantro
1 tablespoon prepared horseradish	Salt and pepper to taste
½ cup bread crumbs	2 tablespoons canola oil

In a mixing bowl combine salmon, mayonnaise, horseradish, beets, cilantro, salt, and pepper with ½ the bread crumbs. Mix well. Measure out 3 tablespoons of the salmon mixture and use your hands to flatten it into a cake. Repeat until you have used up all the salmon mixture. Coat the cakes with the remaining bread crumbs.

Add 2 tablespoons canola oil to a non-stick pan, and pan-fry the cakes over medium heat until crisp and golden brown, or about 2 minutes on each side.

Shrimp Keleguen Cocktail

This is a traditional recipe from Micronesia. The combination of fresh local shrimp, calamansi lime juice, tangerine juice, fresh local turmeric, and toasted coconut gives this shrimp cocktail a deliciously different twist.

—Dean Louie

---

1 pound shrimp (16/20 size), peeled
and de-veined
Juice of 2 tangerines
Juice of 6 Calamansi limes or 2 common
limes
Juice of 2 lemons
1 clove minced garlic
1 tablespoon peeled and minced
turmeric or ginger
Fresh hot chillis to taste, grilled and
finely chopped (I recommend 1-2
jalapeño or Serrano chillis)

2 shallots, minced
Salt and sugar to taste

GARNISHES
Fresh local fruit
Cocktail sauce
Banana chips
Shrimp chips
Tortilla chips
Splash of vodka and/or vermouth
Shredded and toasted fresh coconut
(see page 174 for tips)

Blanch or quickly sauté the shrimp until mostly cooked; this should take about 2 minutes for 16/20 size shrimp. They should just be pink. Do not overcook!

Quickly plunge the shrimp into an ice bath to stop the cooking process. When cool, dry the shrimp well with paper towels. Roughly chop the shrimp and put it in the refrigerator; it should be ice-cold when served.

Combine the fruit juices with the garlic, ginger, chillis, and shallots. Mix to combine and chill.

Drain the shrimp. Add it to the juice mixture and marinate in the refrigerator for at least 30 minutes before serving.

TO SERVE
Carefully adjust the seasonings, using salt and sugar to taste. Serve the shrimp cocktail in martini glasses and garnish with any—or several!—of the garnishes.

'Ōpakapaka Ceviche

This fish dish is one of the most popular appetizers on the menu at our "downtown" restaurant, Mañana Garage. It's light and refreshing, just the thing after a day of active outdoor fun.

Use any fresh white fish, such as onaga, ono, or small sashimi-grade marlin. You can add a few avocado slices to give the salad a creamy accent.

—Eddie Santos

8 ounces 'Ōpakapaka, thinly sliced as for sashimi
¼ cup fresh lime juice
Jicama and Cucumber salad (see page 55)

Hawaiian alaea red sea salt
1 avocado, sliced
4 cilantro sprigs

TO PREPARE THE CEVICHE

In a non-reactive (glass or stainless steel) bowl, place the fish and lime juice. Cover and refrigerate for 20 to 30 minutes. The lime juice "cooks" the fish.

Drain the lime juice from the fish slices. Pour the 4 tablespoons of reserved dressing from the Jicama and Cucumber salad recipe (on page 55) over the fish so that the fish is evenly coated. Season to taste with Hawaiian alaea red sea salt.

TO SERVE

This is best with Jicama and Cucumber Salad (recipe on page 55). Divide the salad between 4 chilled plates. Next to the salad, layer the marinated fish with avocado slices. Garnish with a cilantro sprig.

Rock Shrimp Martini

When fresh rock shrimp come into the restaurant, I can't resist eating a few raw, just to savor their natural sweetness. The taste of raw shrimp inspired me to create a dish that features fresh shrimp, "cooked" lightly with lime juice. It's ceviche with a difference.

—James McDonald

4 pounds fresh rock shrimp
1½ cups fresh lime juice
2 mangoes, diced
1 cup sliced green olives
2 cups red onion, julienned
2 avocados, diced
Lime wedges
¾ cup vodka (your favorite brand)
Coarse sea salt

1 cup extra virgin olive oil
10 cloves roasted garlic
4 Serrano chillies, chopped
2 teaspoons sugar
2 teaspoons kosher salt
1 teaspoon pepper mix (a mix of your
favorites, ground)

OLIVE SWIZZLES
1 pound puff pastry (frozen is fine)
1 cup finely chopped green olives
Egg wash (egg yolk or whole egg
mixed with a little milk)

YELLOW TOMATO COULIS
8 yellow tomatoes, peeled and chopped
6 tablespoons horseradish
1 cup roughly chopped cilantro

TO PREPARE THE COULIS

To peel the tomatoes, see our tips on page 175. Then combine all the coulis ingredients in a food processor and blend to a smooth purée. Chill until ready to serve.

TO PREPARE THE SWIZZLES

If puff pastry is frozen, thaw according to package directions. Lay the puff pastry out on a clean flat surface and spread the chopped olives over the entire surface. Use a rolling pin to flatten the olives into the pastry. You may need to place parchment paper (or waxed paper) over the top to prevent sticking. Cut the pastry into half-inch wide strips and twist them into swizzle sticks. Brush the sticks with egg wash and bake at 350 degrees on a pan lined with parchment paper until golden and crisp, or about 10 minutes.

TO ASSEMBLE THE DISH

Marinate the shrimp in the lime juice for 15 minutes. Drain the shrimp and mix with the tomato coulis. Add the mango, olives, red onion, and avocado. Place in martini glass and serve with lime wedge and Olive Swizzles. Drizzle with vodka and sprinkle with sea salt.

Cured Salmon Gravlax

At our Leis Family Class Act Restaurant, we serve this elegant gravlax appetizer on potato blini, garnished with a bit of chive crème fraîche. It's just as good—and just as elegant—on a crispy crouton or crostini, served with softened cream cheese mixed with capers, chopped red onion, and chopped chives. Fresh salmon is a "must" for this dish.

For a Nuevo Latino flair, try using tequila, lime, and cilantro in place of the gin, lemon juice, and dill. For another tasty variation, brush the cured salmon with molasses and sprinkle some ground pepper and coriander over it. Voila! pastrami-flavored gravlax!

—*Tom Lelli*

1½ pounds salmon fillet, skin on
1 teaspoon lemon juice
1 teaspoon gin
1 piece cheesecloth, enough to wrap twice around the salmon

CURE MIX
1½ cups chopped fresh dill
⅓ cup sugar
1 cup kosher salt
1 teaspoon fresh black pepper, ground coarse
1 tablespoon lemon zest

Mix the ingredients of the cure mix in a medium-size bowl. In a separate bowl, combine the lemon juice and gin. Brush the lemon juice mixture on the salmon. Lay a large piece of cheesecloth on a plate. Place about ⅓ of the cure mix on the center of the cheesecloth. Place the salmon on top of the cure mix, skin side down. Cover the salmon with the remaining cure mix and wrap the salmon tightly in the cheesecloth.

Place the salmon on a wire cooling rack with any pan that has sides under it, to catch the moisture which the cure mix will pull from the fish.

Refrigerate for 36–48 hours. Unwrap the salmon and brush off the cure mix. Blot off any excess moisture with a paper towel. Dry the salmon uncovered in the refrigerator for 2 hours.

Slice paper-thin and serve.

'Ahi Carpaccio

Some of the best 'ahi in world can be found here in Hawai'i. I decided to use this beautiful fish in an elegant appetizer for our Leis Family Class Act Restaurant. The basic idea for this dish came from chef Chris Speere. He was our Class Act instructor way back in the days of our old building.

If you do not have brioche, you can make croutons out of cubed French bread brushed with a little olive oil. If you are adventurous, sprinkle the 'ahi with a few drops of truffle oil.

This dish makes an excellent starter for a special occasion dinner. It's light, easy to prepare ahead of time, and visually stunning. It should be served on large chilled plates.

—Tom Lelli

---

8 ounces sashimi grade 'ahi (center cut or sashimi block)
16 sheets of wax paper, cut into 7 x 7-inch squares
Vegetable pan-release spray
1 cup tender baby herbs (micro herbs) or greens

Olive Relish (see page 15)
Roasted Garlic Aioli (see page 21)
Sea salt
Freshly ground black pepper

CROUTONS
1 loaf brioche or other egg bread

TO PREPARE THE 'AHI

Cut the 'ahi into 8 flat pieces of the same size. Lightly spray 2 sheets of wax paper with vegetable pan-release. Place one piece of 'ahi between the sheets and pound to ⅛-inch thickness with the flat side of a meat mallet or the flat bottom of a small sauté pan. Repeat with the rest of the 'ahi.

TO PREPARE THE CROUTONS

Trim the crust off the brioche with a bread knife. Cut the bread into ¼-inch thick slices and cut those slices into small triangles or rectangles. Place the croutons on an ungreased cookie sheet and toast in a 300 degree oven until the croutons are light brown, dry and crisp. This should take 7–8 minutes. Be sure to check the croutons frequently near the end of the baking to make sure they don't burn.

TO ASSEMBLE THE DISH

Take 2 slices of the thinly pounded 'ahi and remove one (only one!) sheet of wax paper from each slice. Put the 2 pieces of fish in the center of a chilled plate, paperless side down. Carefully pull off the wax paper on top of the fish. Repeat until all the 'ahi has been plated.

Place a spoonful of olive relish on the plate and a drizzle of garlic aioli next to the 'ahi. Garnish with sea salt and freshly ground pepper, and also a pinch of tender baby herbs (micro herbs) or greens. Serve with brioche croutons.

Pan-Seared Shrimp and Pancetta-Wrapped Scallop Skewers

SERVES 10

Shrimp and scallops are featured ingredients in many great seafood recipes. They're delicious plain, but also perform beautifully in more complex recipes. In this recipe, they're paired with vegetables, pancetta, and a flavorful vinaigrette. But the secret to cooking seafood is the same for simple and complicated recipes alike: control your cooking heat so that the seafood browns nicely without overcooking.

Pancetta is an Italian or Spanish dry-cured meat. It's expensive and sometimes hard to find, but the flavor is divine. Use it if you can. Otherwise, you can substitute thin-sliced bacon.

—*Chris Speere*

Bamboo skewers, soaked in water to prevent burning	2 tablespoons finely chopped shallots
20 shrimp (21/25 size), peeled and deveined	3 green zucchinis, julienned
10 scallops (20/30 size)	3 yellow zucchinis, julienned
10 paper-thin slices pancetta, each long enough to wrap around a scallop 1½ times	3 tablespoons finely sliced basil (cut in a chiffonade; see page 175 for tips)
2 tablespoons olive oil	¼ cup dry white wine
	Salt and pepper to taste
	1 cup green onions, julienned
	Tomato Vinaigrette (see page 9)

TO PREPARE THE SKEWERS

Wrap each scallop with a strip of thinly sliced bacon and skewer between 2 shrimp. In a large sauté pan, heat the olive oil over medium-high heat. Cook the skewers quickly, until nicely browned on all sides, or about 2–3 minutes on each side. Remove the skewers from the pan and set them aside.

Add the shallots, zucchini, basil, and white wine to the same sauté pan and cook over medium-high heat for 3–4 minutes, or until the zucchini is tender. Season the vegetables with salt and pepper to taste.

TO ASSEMBLE THE DISH

Put the sautéed vegetables in the center of a serving platter. Place the skewers on top of the vegetables and spoon tomato vinaigrette (see page 9) over the skewers. Garnish the platter with the julienned green onion.

Taro Cakes

Taro is a versatile ingredient—it can be boiled, steamed, baked, or mashed. Here, we use this starchy tuber to make these delicious pan-fried cakes.

We like to serve the taro cakes with the Crispy Moloka'i Prawns on page 92. Or pair them with the Kālua Pork Sandwich on page 69. They are also good on their own as a tasty appetizer.

—Chris Speere

1 pound taro	½ cup chopped green onions
4 tablespoons neutral cooking oil	¼ cup chopped fresh basil
1 cup grated carrots	3 eggs
½ cup diced Maui onions	¼ cup all-purpose flour
1 tablespoon chopped garlic	Salt and pepper to taste
½ cup chopped fresh parsley	

Clean and trim the taro and cut it into medium-size dice, or about ¾-inch squares. Steam taro until soft and thoroughly cooked. Mash taro into a paste and let cool.

Add 2 tablespoons of oil to a hot sauté pan and sauté the carrots, onions, parsley, garlic, and green onions until soft, or about 3–4 minutes.

Place the taro and sautéed vegetables in a large bowl. Add the basil, eggs, flour, salt and pepper, and mix to form a soft dough. Form the taro mixture into 6 cakes.

Heat the sauté pan again, add another 2 tablespoons of oil, and pan-fry the taro cakes for about 2 minutes on each side, or until golden brown.

Moloka'i Sweet Potato Cakes

The Moloka'i sweet potato is known for its vibrant, deep purple color and creamy texture. It is delicious when cooked simply—mashed, grilled, even baked with coconut milk. Or try it in these delicious cakes.

This recipe was created to go with the Soused Opah with Yogurt Sauce on page 114, but they are also wonderful with any other seafood, meat, or poultry entree. They are also excellent as a vegetarian side dish.

—*James McDonald*

1 cup peanut oil
1 large Moloka'i sweet potato, grated
2 tablespoons grated onion
2 tablespoons chopped green onion
1 egg
2 teaspoons flour

¾ teaspoon salt
½ teaspoon pepper
Pinch of nutmeg
1 teaspoon chopped parsley
½ tablespoon lemon juice

In a large frying pan heat the peanut oil over medium heat to 325 degrees.

Combine the rest of the ingredients in a medium size bowl. Mix well, and form into 6 uniform cakes. Pan-fry the cakes in the hot peanut oil for 1½ to 2 minutes per side, or until they are golden brown and crispy. Remove the cakes from the frying pan and let them drain on absorbent paper.

SOUPS, SALADS, SANDWICHES, AND SIDES

At the Maui Culinary Academy, we emphasize the farm-to-table concept in our classroom and dining offerings. Using local produce and market-fresh ingredients supports our growers. But the best reason to buy local? Fresher always tastes better. This section features delectable first courses utilizing our favorite farm-fresh ingredients. We also give familiar favorites, from potato salad to onion rings, a Maui-style twist. Create a stellar meal by mixing and matching these dishes with any favorite *Taste of Maui* entrée.

Kabocha Pumpkin and Toasted Rice Bisque

SERVES 6

Kabocha grows quite well here on Maui and is sold at most local markets; it even grows wild in our family garden. We love our pumpkins grilled, roasted in our pizza oven, or as a filling for homemade ravioli. For this recipe, any pumpkin will do but kabocha pumpkin makes it local. This recipe was passed along to me from John Cox, executive chef of Hotel Hāna-Maui and Honua Spa. As chefs often do, we share recipes to inspire new ideas.

Red Thai curry paste is hot! Add a small amount of the paste at a time until the dish is as hot, or as mild, as you like it.

—Chris Speere

1 kabocha pumpkin (approximately 1 pound)	2 cups unsalted canned chicken broth
1 teaspoon salt	2 cups whole milk
1 teaspoon pepper	½ cup coconut milk
1 tablespoon canola oil	½ cup heavy cream
2 tablespoons unsalted butter	2 tablespoons coconut syrup
½ cup short grain rice	Red chilli oil, to taste (we like Pele's Fire Macadamia Nut Oil)
2 tablespoons minced ginger	2 tablespoons Hawaiian sea salt
2 tablespoons minced lemongrass	1 tablespoon finely chopped fresh basil
½ cup finely diced onion	1 tablespoon finely chopped fresh cilantro
½ to 1 teaspoon red Thai curry paste	1 tablespoon finely chopped fresh mint

Cut the pumpkin in half and remove the seeds. Rub the cavity with salt, pepper, and oil and roast in a 350 degrees oven until the pumpkin meat is soft. This should take approximately 30 minutes. Remove the pumpkin from the oven and scoop out the pumpkin meat.

Melt the butter in a large saucepot over medium heat; add and sauté the rice, ginger, lemongrass, onion, and curry paste. Cook and stir until the ginger and onions have softened and the spices are fragrant; this should take approximately 5 minutes. Stir in the roasted pumpkin meat, the broth, and the milk; simmer the bisque over low heat until the rice is soft, or about 20 minutes.

Purée the bisque in a blender until smooth.

Combine the coconut milk, cream, and coconut syrup in a small bowl.

Ladle the bisque into previously warmed, wide, shallow bowls. Garnish each bowl of bisque with 1 tablespoon of the coconut cream mixture, a drizzle of red chilli oil, and a pinch of sea salt. If desired, top with ½ teaspoon each of the chopped basil, cilantro, and mint.

Maui Corn Chowder

Fresh Maui corn adds the perfect sweetness to this great first course. We recommend using locally-grown corn over canned if possible for the best flavor. To turn this into a hearty meal, serve the chowder with freshly-baked French bread and the Pink Salmon Cakes on page 34.

The flavors in the chowder will intensify overnight, so make a big batch and enjoy it with friends over a weekend.

—*Dean Louie*

---

3 tablespoons butter or cooking oil
1 tablespoon minced garlic
¼ cup finely diced Maui onion
¼ cup finely diced celery
½ cup finely diced mixed red and green bell pepper
3 tablespoons all-purpose flour
1½ quarts fresh milk or reconstituted powdered milk
2 medium potatoes, peeled and cut into ¾-inch dice
1 teaspoon dried thyme

1 teaspoon ground cumin
1 teaspoon ground coriander
5 ears fresh Maui corn, kernels removed (you can substitute 2 cans of corn kernels)
Salt and pepper to taste
Pink salmon cakes (see page 34)
Tender baby mixed herbs (micro herbs) or fresh cilantro (washed, dried, and roughly chopped)
Corn chips or croutons
Crisp bacon, crumbled

TO MAKE THE CHOWDER

In a large saucepan over medium heat, melt the butter and then sauté the garlic, onions, celery, and bell pepper. Cook until the vegetables are slightly wilted, or about 2–3 minutes. Add the flour and blend well. Cook for 3 more minutes. Add the milk, stirring constantly to avoid lumps. Bring to a simmer, then add the potatoes and spices. Cook until the potatoes are tender, or about 8–10 minutes.

Add the corn and season to taste. Keep warm on the stovetop until ready to serve.

TO SERVE

Ladle ¾ cup of corn chowder into each shallow bowl. If using salmon cakes, place in the center, on top of the soup. Garnish with greens, chips or croutons, or bacon crumbles.

Lavender Infused Island Seafood Chowder

I developed this chowder to serve at a recent Noble Grape event, our annual fundraising dinner held at the Fairmont Kea Lani Hotel in Wailea. It was inspired by my time in Boston, where I spent a few years working and enjoying their great food. I loved the New England style chowders and learned to make them while working in the Mount Vernon Restaurant in Somerville, Massachusetts. We always used salt fat back as the basis for the chowders and any mixture of seafood was added to this. Here in Hawai'i, I start my chowder with bacon because it is similar to fat back, yet more available here.

The lavender infused flavors came about through a visit to the Ali'i Kula Lavender farm in upcountry Maui. I loved the aroma and knew that I wanted to use this flavor but it had to be in a recipe where it would complement and not overpower any specific taste. I sensed lavender would go well with cream and butter, so this chowder recipe was born. The lavender in the stock adds a very subtle flavor—too subtle to identify, but definitely there. So for even more lavender punch, I added a lavender infused butter topping, which adds just the right amount of flavor effect.

You can savor the topping by sipping spoonfuls of the chowder without stirring or you can stir the butter right in and savor it throughout. In any case, this is one of my favorite recipes. My validation of this came when my daughter requested this recipe for her high school graduation party!

—*Robert Santos*

LAVENDER SACHET
2 bay leaves
1 teaspoon fresh thyme
1 tablespoon fresh lavender
Cheesecloth and string

LAVENDER BUTTER
2 tablespoons fresh lavender
8 tablespoons butter

ROUX
2 tablespoons butter
2 tablespoons flour

CHOWDER
¼ cup finely diced bacon
¼ cup finely diced onion
¼ cup finely diced celery
¼ cup finely chopped leeks
4 tablespoons butter
2 tablespoons finely chopped garlic
½ cup white wine
2 quarts Fish Stock (see page 7)

2 cups potatoes, diced and blanched
½ cup finely chopped parsley
1 pound island snapper, diced
¼ pound crabmeat, cleaned
½ cup heavy cream
2 tablespoons parsley, finely chopped

(recipe continued on page 50)

TO PREPARE A SACHET

Wrap the bay leaves, lavender, and fresh thyme in cheesecloth and tie with string. Set aside.

TO PREPARE TOPPING

Place lavender and butter together in a sauce pot and heat slowly. Bring the temperature to about 120 degrees and let sit for about 15 minutes. Be careful not to over heat. Strain, then set aside.

TO PREPARE ROUX

Make a roux by stirring two tablespoons of butter with two tablespoons of flour over low heat until blended and smooth for about 1 minute (see page 176 for tips).

TO PREPARE CHOWDER

Melt butter in a heavy bottomed pot. Add bacon, onions, and celery and cook over medium heat for about 6 minutes, stirring frequently. Turn the heat to high and add the garlic and white wine. Let the mixture reduce by 75 percent; this should take about 10 minutes, but time can vary based on source of heat and size of the pot. Add fish stock and sachet, bring to a simmer and let cook for about 20 minutes over low heat.

Add roux and stir to thicken. Add potatoes and parsley, let cook until potatoes are just tender, about 10 minutes. Then add fish and cook for about 5 minutes. Add crabmeat and cream. Stir, then remove from heat.

TO SERVE

Remove the sachet. Divide chowder equally between 8 bowls. Top each serving with 1 tablespoon of lavender butter and sprinkle with chopped parsley.

Creamy Macadamia Nut Seafood Chowder

SERVES 8

This wonderful soup was a staple in the "old" Class Act Restaurant. The old kitchen was extremely small, had no oven, and students had to stand on a five-inch wooden step to reach the gas burners. I think we performed miracles in that kitchen, given the limited space and equipment.

Here on Maui, Kapuna Ranch has wonderful taro. We recommend using what ever is local and fresh at your market. Be sure to thoroughly cook the taro and taro leaf in plenty of boiling water. If you don't, the raw taro will make your throat itch.

—Chris Speere

6 + 6 tablespoons (1½ sticks) butter
½ cup flour
2 cups minced macadamia nuts
1 cup minced onion
1 tablespoon minced garlic
6 cups chicken broth, canned, unsalted
1 cup diced potatoes (¾-inch dice)
4 cups heavy cream
4 cups coconut milk

SEAFOOD GARNISH
4 tablespoons (½ stick) butter
1 cup shrimp (cut into ½-inch pieces)
1 cup scallops (cut into ½-inch pieces)
1 cup fresh snapper (cut into ½-inch pieces)

TARO GARNISH
1 cup julienned cooked taro
2 cups canola oil
1 cup chopped taro leaf
2 teaspoons salt
1 teaspoon white pepper

TO PREPARE THE CHOWDER

In a small saucepot over low heat, melt 6 tablespoons of the butter. Add the flour, and cook and stir for 5 minutes or until the mixture (called a roux; see page 176 for tips) turns a light blond color.

In a large saucepot over medium heat, sauté the macadamia nuts, onions, and garlic in the remaining 6 tablespoons of butter until they are golden brown, for approximately 4 minutes. Whisk in the chicken broth. Bring to a boil and simmer for 10 minutes. Slowly whisk in the roux mixture. Add the diced potatoes, cream, and coconut milk. Season with salt and pepper and simmer an additional 25 minutes.

TO PREPARE THE SEAFOOD GARNISH

While the chowder is simmering in a large sauté pan over medium heat, melt 4 tablespoons butter (listed in garnish ingredients) and sauté the shrimp, scallops, and snapper until completely cooked, for approximately 4 minutes.

(recipe continued on page 52)

Deep fry the julienned taro in the 2 cups of canola oil until it is golden brown and crispy. Set aside on absorbent paper.

Cook the chopped taro leaf in boiling salted water for approximately 15 minutes, drain, and purée it in a blender.

TO SERVE

Set out 8 soup bowls and divide the seafood equally between them. Pour the chowder over the seafood, top with fried taro and drizzle with the taro leaf purée. I garnish each soup bowl separately so that each guest can taste all the ingredients and garnishes.

❀ **SALADS** ❀

Lotus and Asparagus Salad

SERVES 4

I created this dish for our Leis Family Class Act Restaurant when I was still a culinary student at the Maui Culinary Academy. This salad features an unusual and often overlooked vegetable: the lotus root, or hasu as it is known in Japanese. It has a subtle taste and crisp crunch, much like the better-known water chestnut. It can be found in most local grocery stores.

—*Kyle Kawakami*

2 cups peeled, sliced and blanched fresh lotus root	¼ cup sliced green onion
2 cups fresh asparagus tips, blanched	Thinly sliced red and yellow bell peppers (optional)
2 cups fresh watercress	Soy-Ginger Vinaigrette (see page 10)
1 teaspoon black sesame seeds	

TO PREPARE THE LOTUS ROOT

Remove the ends of the lotus root and take off the outer skin with a vegetable peeler. (Note that the lotus root will turn brown if it is not cooked immediately. If you want to prepare it in advance, you should store the peeled root in water mixed with a little lemon juice or vinegar.) Slice the root into thin ⅛ inch rounds. To blanch, stir the sliced lotus root into a large pot filled with 2 quarts of boiling water. Remove the pot from the heat and let it stand for 5 minutes. Drain the lotus root and immediately place it into a large bowl filled with ice water; this stops the cooking process (see page 177 for tips on blanching). Drain the lotus root again and refrigerate it until it is time to serve the salad.

(see page 177 for tips on blanching)

TO PREPARE THE ASPARAGUS AND WATERCRESS

To blanch the asparagus tips, place them in boiling water for approximately 2-3 minutes. Drain the asparagus and immediately place them into the ice water. Drain again and refrigerate until serving time.

Cut watercress into 2-inch lengths. Wash, drain and chill in refrigerator.

TO SERVE

For each individual salad, place 6 pieces of lotus root in a circular pattern on a medium-sized salad plate. Arrange ½ cup of watercress on the center of the lotus root. Arrange 4–6 asparagus tips on top of the watercress. Drizzle salad with dressing, then garnish with sesame seeds, sliced green onions, and thinly sliced bell peppers.

Macadamia Nut, Watercress, and Belgian Endive Citrus Salad

SERVES 4

Geoff Haines of Pacific Produce Incorporated is one of our favorite local suppliers. Pacific Produce grows high quality watercress—hydroponically. The company aims to produce the best possible cress using the least possible land and water, thus conserving precious island resources. Their motto: "Healthy plants equal nutritious healthy food."

Mesclun greens are a mixture of several kinds of salad greens, starting with tender baby lettuce, then accents like oak leaf, romaine and radicchio.

—*Chris Speere*

2 cups julienned Belgian endive	½ pint cherry tomatoes, cut in half
1 cup toasted and chopped macadamia nuts (see page 174 for tips)	2 grapefruits, peeled and segmented
4 cups watercress leaves (no stems)	3 oranges, peeled and segmented
2 cups mixed mesclun greens (or spring greens)	Honey-Citrus Dressing (see page 10)

TO PREPARE THE SALAD

After cutting the endive into julienne matchsticks, soak it in cold water mixed with a little lemon juice or vinegar; this will keep it from browning.

TO SERVE

Before serving, drain the endive, then combine with the watercress, greens and cherry tomatoes. Add the honey-citrus dressing and toss, then sprinkle the salad with toasted macadamia nuts. Garnish with grapefruit and orange segments.

Jicama and Cucumber Salad

Jicama adds a delightful crunch to this refreshing salad. For the best presentation, make sure to julienne the jicama, cucumber, bell pepper, and carrot into uniform shapes.

The salad goes perfectly with my 'Ōpakapaka Ceviche on page 36, or serve it whenever you want a colorful side dish to any entrée.

—Eddie Santos

SALAD
1 cup julienned jicama
1 cup peeled, seeded and julienned cucumber
1 red bell pepper, julienned
1 cup julienned carrot
½ cup whole cilantro leaves (no stalks or roots)
½ cup finely sliced green onions

CITRUS DRESSING
¼ cup lime juice
¼ cup lemon juice
¼ cup orange juice
2 tablespoons honey
2 tablespoons soy sauce
½ teaspoon sesame oil
4 tablespoons olive oil
1 teaspoon chipotle chilli (canned in adobo)
1 teaspoon grated ginger
Salt and pepper to taste

TO PREPARE THE SALAD
Combine all ingredients in a mixing bowl and set aside.

TO PREPARE THE CITRUS DRESSING
Combine all ingredients in a blender and season to taste.

TO ASSEMBLE THE DISH
Set aside 4 tablespoons of citrus dressing to use in the 'Ōpakapaka Ceviche recipe (see page 36). Add the rest of the dressing to the bowl of salad vegetables and toss. Season to taste with salt and fresh ground pepper, then portion the salad evenly onto 4 chilled plates.

Mountain Apple-Watermelon Radish Slaw

Green apples are an excellent substitute for the mountain apples in this recipe. Hawaiian mountain apples resemble a pear more than they do an apple, but for this dish, the acidity of the green apple works better.

Watermelon radish looks just like watermelon when it's sliced: a green rind with a rosy interior. It has a crisp flesh with a mild sweet flavor that's excellent in salads. If you're unable to find watermelon radish, red radish or daikon may be substituted.

I created this side to go with the Bacon-Wrapped 'Ahi entrée on page 127, and the Hana Bay Potato Salad on page 57. But it is also good on its own.

—*John Cox*

---

1 cup julienned mountain apples
½ cup julienned watermelon radish
¼ cup julienned jicama
¼ cup shredded basil (cut in a chiffonade; see page 175 for tips)
¼ cup macadamia nuts, toasted (see page 174 for tips)

SLAW DRESSING
½ cup mayonnaise
4 tablespoons lemon juice
1 tablespoon honey
1 pinch cayenne pepper
2 tablespoons olive oil
Salt

Combine the mountain apples, watermelon radish, jicama, basil, and macadamia nuts in a large bowl and refrigerate. In a small bowl, combine all the dressing ingredients and whisk until incorporated.

Chill the slaw and the dressing in their separate bowls and toss just before serving.

Hana Bay Potato Salad

One of my greatest challenges as a chef is to take an American favorite like potato salad and refine it so that it can take its place on a "fine dining" menu. Potato salad lovers usually have firm opinions as to how this dish should taste and that makes it all the more challenging to exceed the guest's expectations.

I created this side to go with the Bacon-Wrapped 'Ahi entrée on page 127, and the Mountain Apple-Watermelon Radish Slaw on page 56. But it is also good with any meat or seafood dish.

—*John Cox*

2 cups finely diced russet potatoes, raw	Kosher or Hawaiian sea salt to taste
½ cup diced red onion	Black pepper, to taste
¼ cup diced celery	¼ cup mayonnaise
1 tablespoon whole grain mustard	¼ cup minced chives
1 tablespoon lemon juice	¼ cup chopped parsley

Blanch the diced potatoes in 2 quarts of heavily salted boiling water until barely tender, which should take from 1 to 1½ minutes. It's very important not to overcook the potatoes. Drain, put into a pan, and chill in the refrigerator for about 20 minutes.

While the potatoes are chilling, combine the remaining salad ingredients, mix well, and season to taste.

Gently mix the potatoes into the mixture. Chill until it is time to serve.

Chopped Vegetable Salad with Warm Goat Cheese and Beet Vinaigrette

SERVES 6

People often tell me that they never liked beets until they tasted this salad. Roasting the beets caramelizes the beet sugars, making a sweet beet even sweeter. Basil, balsamic vinegar, and olive oil are the supporting flavors here, adding complexity, complementing the basic ingredients and taking a simple dish to a whole new level.

Any variety of beets will work for this salad. I like smaller beets because they are sweeter and less fibrous. As for the accompanying vegetables—if the corn, beans, or bell peppers in your local market are out of season or less than fresh, you can substitute other crisp, sweet, in-season vegetables like asparagus, sugar snap peas, yellow wax beans, zucchini or yellow squash. You could also use any small variety of tomato—like cherry or grape tomatoes—which you do not need to blanch. You can also use your favorite greens for this salad. I like to use some spicy, some bitter, and some soft greens to vary the flavor.

This could be an appetizer for an elegant dinner, or a healthy lunch salad if you add some grilled chicken.

—Tom Lelli

6 red beets, small to medium size, washed	2 tablespoons sherry vinegar
2 sprigs fresh thyme	Salt and fresh ground black pepper
2 ears fresh Maui corn	6 ounces goat cheese (we like the selection from Maui's Surfing Goat Dairy)
1 cup chopped baby green beans	Mixed nuts (such as pistachio, walnuts, macadamia nuts, or pumpkin seeds), toasted and finely chopped
1 red bell pepper, finely diced	
½ cup finely diced red onion	
⅓ cup balsamic vinegar	Thinly sliced red, yellow, and green bell peppers (optional)
3 fresh basil leaves	
1 shallot, peeled and chopped	4 cups arugula or spicy greens, very loosely packed
1 cup extra virgin olive oil (reserve 1 tablespoon for the vegetables)	

TO PREPARE THE BEETS AND VEGETABLES

Preheat oven to 325 degrees. Rub the beets with 2 teaspoons of the olive oil, season with salt and fresh ground pepper, and wrap in a large piece of aluminum foil with the fresh thyme. Bake the beets for approximately 1 hour or until they are tender enough that a small paring knife slides easily into the beets. Remove the beets from the oven and let them cool. If there is any juice left in the foil, reserve it for later use.

Put a large pot of salted water on the stove and bring it to a boil. Blanch the corn in the boiling water for 1 minute and then cool under running water. Cut the corn off the cob into a small stainless steel bowl. Don't throw out the water; leave it simmering on the stove.

When you have finished with the corn, blanch the baby green beans in the water for 30 seconds and place immediately in ice water to stop the cooking process. Drain and cut into small pieces, the same size as the corn kernels.

Peel the cooked beets with a paring knife. Set the skins aside; you will use them later, in the salad dressing. Cut 3 of the beets into small dice. Slice the other 3 beets very thinly and set aside.

If you haven't already cut up the bell pepper and onion, do so now. Put all the cut vegetables, except for the thinly sliced beets, into one bowl. Add the sherry vinegar and the 1 tablespoon of olive oil reserved for the vegetables. Add salt and pepper to taste and toss lightly. Set aside to marinate.

(recipe continued on page 60)

TO PREPARE THE DRESSING

Put ½ cup of the beet skins in a blender or food processor, add 1 cup of water, and blend until smooth. Add the balsamic vinegar, basil, shallot, and the reserved roasted beet juice. Turn on the blender and slowly add the remaining olive oil until the dressing is smooth. Season to taste with salt and fresh pepper.

TO PREPARE THE GOAT CHEESE

Divide the goat cheese into 6 equal parts and roll them into balls. Use the flat of your hand to press each ball into a disc. For a decorative flair, roll the sides of each goat cheese disc into the finely chopped nuts. Place the discs on a pie tin or cookie sheet and set aside at room temperature.

TO SERVE

Divide the thinly sliced beets into 6 portions. Layer them in the center of chilled plates, as shown in the picture. Divide the chopped vegetables into 6 portions. Mound them on top of the sliced beets. Place goat cheese in the oven or under the broiler until slightly warm, or about 30 seconds, and carefully set the cheese on top of the vegetables. For an elegant presentation, serve the greens with beet vinaigrette on a separate platter. To serve the salad family style, arrange the greens around the chopped vegetables and drizzle with beet vinaigrette. If desired, garnish with thinly sliced bell peppers. Serve immediately.

Sesame Cucumber Salad

SERVES 4

This cucumber salad goes perfectly with the 'Ahi Poke recipe on page 26. But it also is nice on its own.

—Dean Louie

1 seedless cucumber, sliced thin	1 teaspoon white sesame seeds,
1 tablespoon kosher salt	toasted and slightly crushed (see
1 tablespoon sugar	page 174 for tips)
2 tablespoon rice wine vinegar	

Toss all the ingredients together; taste and correct the seasoning if necessary. Marinate the salad in the refrigerator for 15–20 minutes.

TO SERVE

Drain the cucumber salad before placing on a plate.

Spinach Salad with Teriyaki 'Ahi, Wasabi Cauliflower, and Lemon Soy Vinaigrette

SERVES 4

Please don't be intimidated by this recipe! It is very easy to prepare and all the ingredients are easily found in our local grocery stores. The results will be well worth your efforts.

—Belia Paul

4 pieces 'ahi (approximately 7 ounces each)

'AHI MARINADE
4 tablespoons soy sauce
4 tablespoons sesame oil
1 tablespoon minced fresh ginger
2 tablespoons rice wine vinegar
1 tablespoon sesame seeds (optional)
1 tablespoon orange juice
3 tablespoons sugar

SPINACH SALAD
4 cups fresh baby spinach, washed well
$\frac{1}{4}$ medium Maui onion or red onion, sliced thin
1 Japanese or regular cucumber, sliced thin
Chives or green onions, sliced thin

WASABI CAULIFLOWER
1 head cauliflower cut into small, equal-size pieces
2 medium russet potatoes, sliced $\frac{3}{4}$-inch thick
2 to 3 tablespoons butter
$\frac{1}{4}$ cup milk
3 tablespoons wasabi powder
Salt and pepper to taste

LEMON SOY VINAIGRETTE
4 tablespoons sesame oil
4 tablespoons fresh lemon juice
4 tablespoons orange juice
1 teaspoon soy sauce
1 teaspoon minced ginger
1 teaspoon minced garlic
2 tablespoons sugar

TO MARINATE THE 'AHI
In a large bowl, combine all the marinade ingredients and mix well. Add the 'ahi, making sure that each piece is well-coated. Marinate in the refrigerator for at least 2 hours, turning the fish occasionally.

TO PREPARE THE SPINACH SALAD
Combine all ingredients in a large bowl and toss.

TO PREPARE THE CAULIFLOWER
Steam or boil the cauliflower and the potatoes for approximately 25 minutes or until soft. Drain and return the vegetables to the pot. Add the butter, milk, and wasabi powder and mash to the consistency of mashed potatoes. Add salt and pepper to taste.

(recipe continued on page 62)

TO PREPARE THE VINAIGRETTE

Combine all ingredients and mix well. The dressing can be kept at room temperature until ready to serve.

TO ASSEMBLE THE DISH

Barbecue or sear the 'ahi in a very hot pan over medium-high heat. Don't overcook; it should still be rare in the middle. Toss the spinach, onion and cucumber with ½ of the lemon soy vinaigrette.

TO SERVE

Divide the salad equally between 4 plates. Place a scoop of wasabi cauliflower on top of the salad and a piece of 'ahi on top of that. Drizzle the remaining dressing over the 'ahi. Sprinkle with chives or green onions and serve.

Maui Roasted Vegetable Salad

Maui nō ka ʻoi—Maui is the best—and we think our island-grown produce is the best, too. We try to use locally grown vegetables exclusively in this dish. They're fresher and more flavorful than those shipped in from other islands or the Mainland.

Of course, if you're cooking this dish and you don't live on Maui, use the best local produce you can find. Being a "locavore" is a more environmentally kind and less expensive way to cook and eat. We encourage all of you to eat locally, wherever you live.

The salad goes well with the Thai Basil Beef entrée on page 128.

—Chris Speere

2 Maui onions, peeled and sliced thin

2 Japanese eggplants, peeled, split lengthwise, and then cut into 1-inch chunks

30 large asparagus spears, whole

6 green onions, cut into 1-inch pieces

1 large kabocha pumpkin, peeled and cut into 1-inch chunks

2 bell peppers (any color), julienned

½ cup canola oil

3 tablespoons minced garlic

½ cup dry white wine

Salt and pepper

DRESSING

½ cup olive oil

⅓ cup lemon juice

¼ cup red wine vinegar

2 tablespoons finely chopped green onion

2 cloves garlic, minced

2 tablespoons chopped Thai basil

1 tablespoon chopped flat leaf parsley

Preheat the oven to 375 degrees. Put the onions, eggplant, asparagus, green onions, pumpkin, and bell peppers in a large mixing bowl, add the canola oil, wine, and garlic, and mix well. Season with salt and pepper.

Arrange the vegetables in a single layer in a large pan and pour any remaining liquid over them. Roast the vegetables in the oven for 35 minutes or until tender. Remove the roasted vegetables from the oven and toss them with the dressing ingredients.

Serve on a large platter family-style.

Spicy Calamari and Chickpea Salad

This dish is a warm salad, featuring tomatoes, peppers, herbs, and hot sautéed calamari. You'll savor the play of temperatures (hot and cold) and textures (smooth, soft, and chewy). The salad is wonderfully complemented by a glass of chilled Chardonnay.

—Chris Speere

2 pounds squid, cleaned and cut into rings, tentacles left whole
1 medium red onion, finely diced
1 cup finely diced celery
2 jalapeño peppers, seeded and finely diced
3 tablespoons chopped garlic
2 cups finely diced local ripe tomatoes (seeded)
1 cup white wine (Chardonnay is best here)
1 teaspoon lime zest
3 tablespoons chopped fresh parsley
1 teaspoon finely chopped fresh chives
Salt and pepper to taste

Olive oil as needed
2 cups canned chickpeas, drained and rinsed

SALAD
2 heads of red leaf or butter lettuce, washed and cut into halves

DRESSING
2 tablespoons lemon juice
1 teaspoon Dijon mustard
1 teaspoon chopped fresh basil
4 tablespoons extra virgin olive oil
Salt and pepper to taste

TO PREPARE THE DRESSING

Put the lemon juice, mustard, and basil in a stainless steel bowl. Mix in the olive oil with a wire whisk and season with salt and pepper.

TO PREPARE THE CALAMARI

Heat 2 tablespoons of olive oil in a large pot or sauce pan over medium-high heat. Add the onion and sauté over medium heat for 2 minutes. Add the celery, peppers, and ½ of the garlic. Sauté the mixture over medium heat until aromatic, or about 3 minutes, and set aside.

Dry the squid on some paper towels and season with salt and pepper. In another sauté pan, heat 2 tablespoons of olive oil over high heat. Cook the squid, the remaining garlic, and the tomatoes in the olive oil for 2 minutes, then deglaze the pan with white wine. Turn the heat down to medium-low and slowly reduce the liquid by ½. This should take approximately 2–3 minutes. Add the cooked vegetables, lime zest and herbs. Cook the entire mixture over medium heat for another 2 minutes. Season with salt and pepper and set aside.

TO SERVE
Place ½ head of red leaf or butter lettuce on each plate. Pour the dressing over the lettuce and garnish with chickpeas. Spoon warm calamari and vegetables around the salad and serve.

Roasted Five-Spice Chicken Salad

This dish was developed and served in the summer of 2002, during a training program for Hawai'i Department of Education School Lunch Program Food Service Managers. We were helping them create new menus. This recipe was a standout. The flavors were familiar, the salad was easy to prepare, and it was full of fresh and colorful ingredients.

This salad is best served immediately after it is tossed with the dressing.

—*Chris Speere*

CHICKEN AND MARINADE
1 whole chicken (approximately 2½ pounds)
¼ cup canola oil
2 tablespoons soy sauce
3 tablespoons minced ginger
3 tablespoons minced garlic
2 tablespoons honey
2 teaspoons turmeric powder
1½ teaspoon Chinese five-spice powder
1 teaspoon salt
1 tablespoon olive oil

SALAD
2 cups chopped Napa cabbage, cleaned and cut into bite size pieces
1 cup julienned jicama
1 cup julienned red bell pepper
1 cup thinly sliced red onion
1 cup blanched and julienned snow peas
½ cup diced canned lychee fruit
¼ cup chopped fresh cilantro leaves

½ cup sliced green onions, cut on bias
1 cucumber, halved and thinly sliced (optional)

DRESSING
6 tablespoons oyster sauce
4 tablespoons red wine vinegar
2 teaspoons Dijon mustard
1 tablespoon minced ginger
1 teaspoon chopped garlic
1 cup canola oil
2 teaspoons black pepper
2 teaspoons white sesame seeds
2 teaspoons black sesame seeds
1 teaspoon salt

½ cup sliced almonds, toasted (optional; see page 174 for tips)
4 plantain chips (slice 1 plantain lengthwise and deep fry until golden brown)
4 cilantro sprigs

TO PREPARE THE CHICKEN

Combine all the chicken marinade ingredients in a medium-size bowl. Stir well to blend. Coat your hands with olive oil and massage the chicken all over with the marinade. Put the chicken in a pan, cover and marinate overnight in the refrigerator.

Preheat oven to 450 degrees. Line a rimmed baking sheet or roasting pan with aluminum foil. Place the chicken, breast side up, on the foil. Roast the chicken at 450

(recipe continued on page 68)

degrees for 25 minutes. Reduce the heat to 375 degrees and continue roasting chicken for approximately 35 minutes, or until the chicken juices run clear when a sharp knife is stuck into the thigh meat. Remove the chicken from the oven and it set aside to cool at room temperature for approximately 30 minutes. Using a fork, shred the chicken into bite size pieces. Set aside until you are ready to assemble the salad.

TO PREPARE THE SALAD AND DRESSING

In large bowl toss all the salad ingredients together. Mix well to blend. Refrigerate the salad until you are ready to serve.

In a blender, purée the oyster sauce with the vinegar, mustard, ginger, and garlic. With the blender still running, add the canola oil in a slow steady stream. Blend until the dressing is thick and creamy. Add the pepper, sesame seeds, and the salt; blend briefly. The dressing can be made ahead of time and stored in a jar in the refrigerator.

TO SERVE

Combine the shredded chicken with the salad ingredients (and cucumber, if using) in a large bowl. Add the dressing, toss well, and adjust the seasoning if necessary. Divide the chicken salad into 4 equal portions and place on 4 plates. Garnish each serving with 1 plantain chip, cilantro sprig, and if desired, toasted sliced almonds.

Tropical Fruit Salad
with Yogurt Mint Dressing

SERVES 4

A refreshing fruit salad for our warm Maui days. Tropical flavors pair with the bright clean tastes of mint and yogurt in this simple yet elegant salad.

You can vary this salad with other fresh fruits; orange segments, seedless grapes, melons, strawberries and blueberries work particularly well. Just be sure that the fruits are fresh and high quality.

—Darryl Dela Cruz

2 whole Maui Gold pineapples (leave the tops on)	½ cup pineapple or grapefruit juice
	½ cup plain nonfat yogurt
2 cups diced mango, cut into ½-inch cubes	2 tablespoons chopped fresh mint
	2 tablespoons honey
2 cups diced papaya, cut into ½-inch cubes	1 tablespoon fresh lime juice
	2 kiwi fruits, peeled and sliced
16 grapefruit segments	2 teaspoons poppy seeds
16 whole fresh lychees	4 mint sprigs

Cut the fresh pineapple in half. Hollow out the pineapple halves using a sharp paring knife, removing the fruit in the largest pieces you can manage. You can either use or discard the core, depending on your own taste. Chop the fruit into ½-inch cubes. (It's up to you whether you use the pineapple core or not; some people like the core, some people don't.) Save the empty pineapple halves to use as serving dishes.

In a medium-size mixing bowl, gently mix the mango, pineapple, papaya, grapefruit, lychees, and the juice.

Prepare the dressing by whisking the yogurt, mint, honey, and lime juice together.

TO SERVE

Fill each pineapple half with ½ of the tossed fruit salad. Arrange the kiwi slices in an attractive pattern on top of the salad, then drizzle the dressing over the fruit. Garnish with poppy seeds and mint sprigs.

❀ SANDWICHES ❀

Kālua Pork Sandwich

SERVES 4

We give a flavorful twist to a traditional Hawaiian dish—kālua pork—by serving it as a sandwich. The green onion pesto adds an island-style kick and is very flavorful. This dish is extremely popular at our Paniolo Grill.

We use Napa cabbage in this recipe because it tastes sweeter than regular head cabbage. You can use any sandwich bun you like. Herbed Kaiser rolls, sesame seed rolls, or taro buns work especially well. Serve with taro chips for a perfect lunch. Or skip the bun altogether and serve with the Taro Cakes on page 43 for an entrée-style dish.

—*Darryl Dela Cruz*

1½ pound pork shoulder
1 tablespoon liquid smoke
1 tablespoon kosher or coarse salt
¼ cup vegetable oil (for browning the pork)
Beef stock, as needed; canned is fine
4 sandwich buns

SAUTÉED CABBAGE
2 tablespoons vegetable oil (for cooking the cabbage)
2 cups thinly sliced Napa cabbage
1 teaspoon caraway seeds

Green Onion Pesto (see page 15)

(recipe continued on page 70)

TO PREPARE THE PORK

Preheat the oven to 350 degrees. With a small, sharp paring knife cut 12, equally spaced, ½-inch deep slices on the surface of the pork shoulder. Rub with liquid smoke and salt. Let the pork marinate for 1 hour.

Heat the ¼ cup of oil in a medium, straight-sided fry pan over medium-high heat until it is smoking. Add the pork and brown on all sides, for approximately 4 minutes per side. Add enough beef stock to reach halfway up the pork. Bring to a boil.

Turn off the heat, cover the pan, and immediately place it in the oven. Cook until the pork is very tender, or about 2 hours. When the pork is done, remove it from pan. Strain the braising liquid. Place the strained liquid in a saucepot and lightly boil it over medium heat until the liquid is reduced by ½. This should take 10 to 15 minutes. The finished sauce should be a thin syrup. Pull the pork into shreds with two forks or two sets of tongs and keep warm.

TO PREPARE THE CABBAGE

Heat the 2 tablespoons of oil in a sauté pan over medium heat. Add the sliced cabbage and caraway seeds. Cook and stir until the cabbage and caraway seeds develop a strong aroma, or about 2 minutes. Add the braising liquid and simmer the cabbage until tender, which may take 5 minutes or so. Set aside and keep warm.

TO ASSEMBLE THE DISH

If the sandwich buns aren't already split, split them now. Heat the split buns on a grill or toast them lightly. Spread the green onion pesto on both non-crust sides of the buns. Spread each of the bottom halves with ¼ of the braised cabbage; top the cabbage with 4 ounces of the shredded pork. Cover each sandwich with the top half of its roll and serve.

Asian Flank Steak Sandwich with Green Bell Peppers, Onions, and Mushrooms

This is a simple dish, but it delivers a spectacular burst of Asian flavor and texture. Serve it with any of your favorite sandwich side dishes: French fries, a tossed green salad, even kim chee. Or try it with Paniolo Grill's Onion Rings on page 75.

As an alternative to the sandwich, serve the flank steak and vegetables with rice for a simple and delicious entrée.

—Darryl Dela Cruz

---

1 pound flank steak
4 French baguettes (6-inch long), split
Sesame oil to taste
Chopped green onions

MARINADE AND SAUCE
½ cup soy sauce
½ cup sugar
1 tablespoon sliced ginger
1 teaspoon sliced garlic
½ cup water
2 green onions, sliced

CORNSTARCH SLURRY
2 tablespoons cornstarch
2 tablespoons cold water

ASIAN VEGETABLE TOPPINGS
2 tablespoons hoisin sauce
2 tablespoons soy sauce
1 tablespoon chilli garlic sauce
2 tablespoons peanut or canola oil
½ cup thinly sliced green peppers
½ cup thinly sliced onion
½ cup thinly sliced mushrooms
½ teaspoon minced garlic, minced
Salt and pepper to taste

TO PREPARE THE MARINADE

In a medium-size mixing bowl, combine the soy sauce, sugar, ginger, garlic, water, and green onions. Mix well to dissolve the sugar. Reserve ¼ of this marinade for the sauce. Marinate the flank steak overnight in the refrigerator.

Put the rest of the marinade into a sauce pan. Heat it to a simmer over medium-low heat. Combine the cornstarch and water in a small mixing bowl to create a cornstarch slurry (see page 176 for tips). Add the cornstarch slurry to the simmering sauce and cook until the sauce thickens, or about 3–5 minutes. Strain the sauce through a strainer or sieve into a small saucepot and keep warm.

(recipe continued on page 72)

TO PREPARE THE STEAK

Remove the flank steak from the marinade. Heat a grill pan over medium heat, or fire up your barbecue. Place the flank steak on the hot grill or barbecue and cook 5-8 minutes per side, or until the steak reaches medium doneness. Remove the steak from the heat and put it on a large platter. Let the meat rest for 10 minutes then, cutting against the grain, slice the steak into 2½-inch wide pieces. Cut these against the grain again into small ¼-inch slices. Keep the slices warm until you are ready to assemble the sandwiches.

TO PREPARE THE VEGETABLES

In a small bowl, combine the hoisin sauce, soy sauce, and chilli garlic; mix until well combined. Set aside.

In a sauté pan over medium-high heat, heat the peanut or canola oil until it starts to smoke. Add the peppers and onions and cook for 1 minute. Add the mushrooms and garlic and stir-fry for 1 more minute. Finally, add the hoisin mixture to the vegetables and stir-fry for 1 minute. Keep warm.

TO ASSEMBLE THE SANDWICHES

Brush the non-crust sides of the split baguettes with sesame oil. Place all the split baguettes, non-crust side down, on the hot grill and cook them until they are lightly toasted; this should take no more than 1 minute. Set out 4 plates and put one of the bottom halves of the baguettes on each plate. Top each half-baguette with ¼ of the sliced steak, then ¼ of the vegetable garnish. Drizzle the reserved sauce over the vegetables and steak, then finish with the top halves of the baguettes. Garnish with chopped green onions.

Herb-grilled Garden Vegetable Wrap with Basil Mayonnaise and Balsamic Glaze

This is an all-time favorite at our Paniolo Grill, for vegetarians and meat-eaters alike. This veggie wrap highlights Maui's best produce, and is so full of flavor that it can hold its own among our meat and poultry dishes. To add an extra layer of character to this already tasty wrap, serve it with your favorite dip. I often serve it with roasted garlic or roasted ancho chilli dipping sauce.

You can substitute dried parsley, thyme, and oregano for the fresh herbs. If you do, use ⅓ of the quantities listed in the recipe. You can add grilled chicken or beef to the wrap if you simply must have your meat.

—Darryl Dela Cruz

1 zucchini, sliced lengthwise, about ⅛-inch thick
1 yellow squash, sliced lengthwise, about ⅛-inch thick
1 large eggplant, sliced lengthwise, about ⅛-inch thick
¼ cup coarse salt
1½ large tomatoes, sliced ¼-inch thick
1 large Maui onion, sliced into ¼-inch thick rings
1½ cups sliced white mushrooms
Olive oil as needed
1 tablespoon minced garlic

¼ cup minced fresh parsley
2 teaspoons minced fresh thyme
2 teaspoons minced fresh oregano
2½ teaspoons salt
2½ teaspoons ground black pepper
½ cup balsamic vinegar
4 tablespoons grated Parmesan cheese
4 flour tortilla wraps

BASIL MAYONNAISE
¼ cup basil, chopped
4 tablespoons olive oil
¼ cup mayonnaise

TO PREPARE THE VEGETABLES

Lay out the long thin slices of eggplant in a flat pan. Sprinkle both sides of the eggplant with salt. Lay a piece of parchment paper on the eggplant, then set another flat pan on top of that. Place something heavy on the topmost pan. Set your improvised eggplant press aside for 20 minutes or so.

In the meantime, coat the sliced zucchini, yellow squash, tomato, onions and mushrooms with the olive oil. Toss the vegetables with the garlic, parsley, thyme, oregano, salt, and pepper. Set aside.

(recipe continued on page 74)

After the eggplant has been pressed for 20 minutes, remove the eggplant slices, wash off the salt, and dry them between paper towels. Add the eggplant to the marinating vegetable mixture. Toss well to coat the eggplant with the herbs. Set aside.

TO PREPARE THE BALSAMIC GLAZE

Place the balsamic vinegar in a saucepot and heat to a simmer over medium heat. Cook until the vinegar is syrupy (this is called reducing the vinegar) for 10–15 minutes. Place the balsamic syrup in a squirt bottle and set aside.

TO MAKE THE MAYONNAISE

Combine the basil and olive oil in a blender. Purée until the mixture is smooth. Combine the basil mix with the mayonnaise and store the mixture in the refrigerator until you are ready to use it.

TO GRILL THE VEGETABLES

Heat a grill pan over medium heat, or, heat up your barbecue. Place the sliced eggplant, squash, zucchini, and onion on the grill and cook them for 3-4 minutes. Turn them over, to cook the other side; then add the sliced tomatoes and mushrooms to the grill. You are adding them later because they take less time to cook. Continue cooking for another 3-5 minutes, or until all the vegetables are tender. Remove the vegetables from the grill, put them in a medium bowl, and keep warm. Leave the grill on.

TO ASSEMBLE THE WRAPS

Put the tortilla wraps on the grill and heat until warm, watching closely so that they don't burn. When they are ready, remove them from the grill and wrap them in a sheet of aluminum foil to keep them warm.

Spread each warmed tortilla with 1½ tablespoons of basil mayonnaise on the bottom ⅓ of the wrapper. On top of the mayonnaise, form ¼ of the grilled vegetable mixture into a straight line. Drizzle the vegetable mix with the balsamic glaze, then sprinkle with 1 tablespoon of parmesan cheese. Starting from the bottom, roll the wrapper towards the top. Tuck in the sides as you roll; this totally encloses the food and forms an attractive clean roll. Slice the roll in half, cutting on the diagonal.

Paniolo Grill's Onion Rings

I've eaten onion rings for years, but in all that time, I never really tasted the onions! I wanted to taste more than the batter, so I came up with my own recipe. You'll find that this light but rich batter accents the flavors of the onions without masking them. It makes our sweet Maui onions even sweeter.

Onion rings cook best when they are frozen. Don't use the inner part of the onion (the smaller rings); you'll end up with a clump of batter rather than a ring. For more tips on deep frying, see page 177.

These rings taste great as a side dish with any sandwich or at any backyard barbecue. Serve with your favorite condiments.

—Darryl Dela Cruz

---

2 large Maui onions, sliced into ¼-inch thick rounds

BATTER
1½ cups all-purpose flour
1 teaspoon salt
6 tablespoons sugar
1½ teaspoons baking soda
1 tablespoon baking powder
1 cup milk or buttermilk

¼ cup 7UP soda or club soda
1 egg, lightly beaten
1 tablespoon butter, melted

FOR DREDGING
2 cups all-purpose flour
2 cups panko (Japanese breadcrumbs)
1 quart vegetable oil for deep frying
Salt to taste

TO MIX THE BATTER

Sift together the flour, salt, sugar, baking soda, and baking powder in a large mixing bowl. In a separate bowl, whisk together the milk, soda, egg and melted butter. Add the wet ingredients to the dry, and stir with a whisk or use your hand to mix the batter. It should be slightly lumpy.

TO PREP THE ONION RINGS

Dredge the sliced onions in the additional 2 cups of flour, make sure that they're well coated, with no bare spots. Shake the rings to remove the excess flour. Dip the rings into the batter and let the excess drip off. Dredge in the panko. Again, make sure that they're well coated, with no bare spots. Place the panko-covered onion rings in a pan and freeze until hard, or about 3 hours.

(recipe continued on page 76)

Note: You can make a large batch of these and freeze them in plastic bags—get as much air out of the bags as you can. They will keep for up to three weeks and longer if kept in vacuum sealed bags.

TO FRY THE ONION RINGS

When the onion rings are frozen and you are ready to fry the onion rings, pour the oil into a large heavy bottom saucepot. Heat the oil to 350 degrees. It's always a good idea to check the temperature of cooking oil with a kitchen thermometer to ensure proper cooking. When the oil reaches the correct temperature, add the onion rings. Be sure not to overcrowd the pot. Fry until golden brown, or about 1 minute on each side. Drain the onion rings on paper towels and season with salt.

Maui Asparagus Parmigiana

SERVES 6 AS A SIDE DISH

Maui farmers, such as Bill Mertens of Anuhea Farm in Makawao, grow sweet, delicious asparagus. This easy dish brings out the best in this Maui specialty.

—Chris Speere

1 pound fresh asparagus	1 to 1½ tablespoons lemon juice
Pinch of salt	2 teaspoons extra virgin olive oil
¼ cup freshly-grated Parmesan cheese	Freshly ground black pepper

Preheat oven to 350 degrees.

Fill a large pot two with 8 quarts of cold water. Bring to a boil and add salt. Blanch the asparagus for 2 minutes. Immediately rinse the asparagus in cold water to stop the cooking process. Drain it well.

Place the asparagus in a baking dish and sprinkle with Parmesan cheese. Drizzle with the lemon juice and olive oil over the asparagus. Top with freshly ground pepper. Bake for 5–7 minutes, until the cheese is melted and the dish is piping hot. Serve immediately.

TO SERVE

Serve family-style on a platter, with thin lemon slices garnishing the asparagus spears.

Calabacita

This is a Latin-accented vegetable stew, spiked with cilantro, lime and crumbled Mexican cheese. The dish is inspired by Maui's growing Latin American and Mexican communities. We serve the Calabacita with Cumin Crusted 'Ahi and Lamb Chops with Mole Rub in our Leis Family Class Act Restaurant. It works well as a side dish with most hearty fish or meat dishes. It's particularly good when made with fresh summer vegetables. Any leftovers are a great filling for omelets. Plus, it's healthy too!

Cook the calabacita just before serving, so that the flavors are fresh and the vegetables are al dente crisp.

You can substitute feta cheese if queso blanco is unavailable.

—Tom Lelli

---

2 tablespoons olive oil	1 cup finely diced tomato
2 cloves garlic, minced	Juice of 1 lime
½ cup finely diced red onion	½ cup tomato juice
½ cup finely diced green chilli (Anaheim or Poblano)	½ cup chopped cilantro
1 cup finely diced zucchini	½ cup grated Queso Blanco (crumbly Mexican cheese)
1 cup finely diced yellow squash	Salt and fresh ground pepper
1 cup fresh corn kernels	

In large sauté pan, heat the olive oil over medium heat. Add the garlic, red onion and chillis. Sauté for 1 minute or until fragrant. Do not allow the ingredients to brown. Add the zucchini, yellow squash, corn, and tomato. Season with salt and pepper. Sauté for 1 minute more, then add the lime and tomato juices. Simmer for 2 minutes, being careful not to overcook. The vegetables should have their original colors and should not be too soft.

Sprinkle with cheese and cilantro before serving.

Hot Garlic Eggplant

Eggplant is a delicious vegetable that doesn't get the attention it deserves. It can be cooked in so many ways and enhanced with so many different flavorings. In this recipe, we use Asian cooking techniques and condiments to prepare a spicy eggplant dish that is both crispy and creamy.

If you like "hot," add more garlic chilli paste—a little at a time, please, as it's fiery stuff.

—*Ben Marquez*

---

4 cups peeled and sliced Japanese eggplant (cut in half lengthwise, then into ½-inch slices)
3 cups + ⅓ cup vegetable oil
1 tablespoon chopped garlic
1 teaspoon chopped ginger
4 stalks of green onion sliced on the bias (reserve 1 for garnish)
½ cup julienned red bell pepper
½ cup julienned green bell pepper
¼ cup soy sauce
½ cup oyster sauce
2 tablespoons rice wine vinegar
½ cup brown sugar
2 tablespoons red garlic chilli paste
Sesame seeds, toasted (see page 174 for tips)

In a large, heavy pot over medium heat, bring the 3 cups of oil to 350 degrees. Use a frying thermometer to gauge the heat. Fry the eggplant in small batches until it is golden brown, or approximately 2 minutes per batch. Drain the eggplant on paper towels and keep it warm in a large covered bowl.

Heat the remaining ⅓ cup of oil in a sauté pan over medium heat. Add the garlic, ginger, and green onions and sauté until golden brown, about 3 minutes. Add the bell peppers, soy sauce, oyster sauce, rice wine vinegar, sugar, and chilli paste. Cook over medium heat for an additional 5 minutes. Remove from heat and pour the vegetable sauce over the eggplant. Toss thoroughly.

TO SERVE

Serve family style on a large platter. You can garnish the dish with sliced green onions and toasted sesame seeds.

Sautéed Swiss Chard with Bacon, Garlic, and Toasted Macadamia Nuts

SERVES 6 AS A SIDE DISH OR 4 AS AN ENTRÉE

I often sauté hearty greens like Swiss chard, kale or mustard greens in a neutral-flavored broth. The natural flavors of the greens infuse the cooking broth, capturing the true essence of each vegetable.

Swiss chard comes in a variety of intense colors, making this dish a beautiful accent to a meal.

—Chris Speere

¼ cup olive oil	Salt and freshly cracked black pepper
½ cup bacon, diced into ½-inch pieces	(see page 174 for tips)
1 medium onion, cut into ⅛-inch slices	2 tablespoons fresh lemon juice
4 garlic cloves, peeled and chopped	2 tablespoons chopped flat leaf parsley
1/4 teaspoon red chilli flakes	½ cup chopped and toasted macadamia
1½ pounds Swiss chard, thick stems	nuts (see page 174 for tips)
removed, sliced into 2-inch lengths	1 teaspoon grated lemon zest
¾ cup vegetable or chicken broth	Olive oil

TO PREPARE THE VEGETABLES

In a large sauté pan over medium-high heat, heat the ¼ cup olive oil. Add the bacon and cook until browned, stirring constantly, for about 2 minutes. Add onions, garlic, and chilli flakes and cook another minute. Add the Swiss chard and cook for 2 additional minutes. Add the broth and simmer until the chard is tender, approximately 10 minutes. Season with salt, pepper and lemon juice.

TO SERVE

Garnish with chopped flat leaf parsley, toasted macadamia nuts, and grated lemon zest.

Serve family-style on a platter with a light drizzle of olive oil.

Mushroom Risotto

SERVES 4

Next to paella, risotto is my favorite rice dish. Italian risotto is quite different from the rice we eat regularly in Hawai'i. It is a complete meal in itself. For the best results use Italian rice. It can be found in gourmet shops or ordered over the Internet. Short grain rice can be used in a pinch if you cannot find Italian rice.

Risotto can be flavored with many different ingredients. If you do not like mushrooms, use tomatoes, garlic and shrimp. Risotto is easier to make than most people think, so your friends and family will be pleased and impressed if you take the time to try this recipe.

You can make the dish richer if you add a dash heavy cream, but it's good without the cream too. Try using a mix of the different fresh mushrooms available, such as shiitakes, portabellas, white mushrooms, and porcinis. If you cannot find dried wild mushrooms, use dried shiitake to flavor the stock. Try keeping the chicken stock hot on the stove while you prepare the mushrooms, onions, and rice; it will save you some time.

Risotto can be a meal by itself when accompanied by a light salad. It can also be a rich side dish for a meat, poultry, or fish entrée.

—*Tom Lelli*

1 cup dried porcini mushrooms	1 cup sliced fresh mushrooms (any variety)
1 quart chicken stock	
1 cup dried wild mushrooms or dried shiitake mushrooms	1½ cups Italian Arborio, Vialone, or Carnaroli rice
4 tablespoons + 4 tablespoons butter (1 stick)	⅓ cup dry white wine
1 cup finely chopped onion	1½ cups grated Parmesan cheese
	1 bunch Italian parsley, chopped
	Salt and fresh ground pepper

Bring the chicken stock to a boil. Remove it from the heat and steep the dried porcini and dried shiitake mushrooms in the chicken stock for 15 minutes. Strain the stock and reserve it in a pot on the stove to keep it warm. Rough chop and reserve the reconstituted mushrooms. You will need to remove the stems from the shiitake mushrooms, as they are too woody to eat.

In a preheated heavy-bottom saucepan over medium heat, melt 4 tablespoons of butter. Add the onions and the fresh mushrooms and sauté until soft, or about 5 minutes. Add 2 more tablespoons of butter to the pan and then add the rice. Stirring constantly, sauté over medium heat until the rice emits a nutty fragrance, or approximately 5 minutes. Add the wine and continue stirring until all the liquid has evaporated.

Then start adding hot chicken broth one ladle at a time, stirring the rice until each ladle of liquid is absorbed. The rice will "fizz" when the stock is added, but should not be kept at a constant boil as you do this. Halfway through this process—after you've ladled in ½ of the chicken stock—add all the reconstituted mushrooms. Season lightly with salt and pepper; you can correct the seasoning after the rice is done. Do not over-salt now, as you will be adding salty Parmesan cheese later. Continue adding stock until you have used it all.

When the rice is al dente and creamy, add the Parmesan cheese and the remaining 4 tablespoons of butter. It will take approximately 20 minutes for the rice to reach the al dente stage; you'll want to cook it for 5 more minutes if you prefer your rice softer.

Taste the risotto and correct the seasoning if necessary. Garnish with chopped parsley and serve.

Velvety Smooth Yukon Gold Potato and Parsnip Purée

SERVES 6

I love the sweetness of Yukon Gold potatoes; the parsnip adds another dimension of flavor. This dish goes well with just about anything, but I particularly like it with seared salmon. I use a ricer for the potatoes, which results in an ultra smooth texture. Each bite will melt in your mouth. For an even more velvety texture, push the purée through a fine tamis or drum sieve.

—*Tom Lelli*

5–6 medium-size Yukon gold potatoes, peeled, cut into 1-inch cubes	½ cup heavy cream (optional)
1½ cups peeled and cubed parsnip (cut into 1-inch cubes)	12 tablespoons (1½ sticks) butter, room temperature
	Salt and fresh ground white pepper

Place potatoes in a pot and cover them with cold water. Place the parsnip cubes in a separate small pot and cover them with cold water. Over medium heat, bring the potatoes and parsnips to a simmer. Cook both the potatoes and the parsnips for about 10 minutes, until tender. Do not overcook. Drain the potatoes and parsnips in a colander and let stand for 5 minutes.

(recipe continued on page 82)

Run the warm potatoes and parsnip through a potato ricer or food mill. Warm the cream in a small saucepan. Mix the butter and heavy cream into the potato purée and season with salt and white pepper. Keep warm until ready to serve.

Creamy Cheesy Polenta

SERVES 6

Creamy polenta is a great comfort food. Try it with braised meats and stews in place of mashed potatoes. This particular creamy dish is also delicious served simply with fresh tomato sauce or oven-dried tomatoes (see page 2).

You can replace the Jack cheese with your favorite soft, creamy cheese. Use Reggiano Parmesan if you can—it's the best. For a different twist, add your favorite blue cheese and fresh thyme. If you add more polenta meal to the recipe, the result is a thicker polenta that can be spread out on a cookie sheet, cooled, and cut into squares for grilling, sautéing, or baking.

—*Tom Lelli*

1 quart chicken stock	2 cups grated jack cheese
1 cup whole milk	½ cup grated Parmesan (make sure it's
1½ cups fine or medium-grain polenta	high-quality cheese)
4 tablespoons butter, softened	Salt and pepper

In a heavy saucepot over medium heat, bring chicken stock and milk to a simmer. Reduce heat to low and slowly stir in the polenta. Stirring constantly, simmer for 7–10 minutes or until the polenta thickens to the consistency of cake batter. If it's too thick, add a little more stock or milk.

Stir in butter and cheeses until combined evenly throughout the polenta. Season with salt and pepper and serve.

ENTRÉES

Maui is a melting pot of cultures, and the dishes in this section reflect many international influences on our cuisine. From familiar Asian ingredients to traditional Hawaiian flavors to classical European culinary techniques—and sometimes, all combined in one recipe!—we've got something to please any palate. Our chefs show how easy it is to create stunning main courses and creative, sophisticated fare with step-by-step instructions. Each world-class dish can be plated with elegance or dished out family-style. We're sure you'll enjoy this culinary trip around the world.

Pad Thai Tofu

SERVES 6

This popular Thai dish is found on most Thai restaurant menus; of course, we think our version is a winner. This pad Thai is cooked vegetarian-style, but you if you want, you can easily add shrimp or thinly sliced chicken. If you do not have a large wok or sauté pan, stir-fry the noodles in two batches.

You can buy the tamarind paste in the Asian section of many regular supermarkets, Asian markets, specialty markets, or over the Internet.

—Tom Lelli

---

2 packages (12 to 16 ounces) of Thai rice noodles
½ cup tamarind paste
¾ cup warm water
4 tablespoons fish sauce
3 tablespoons sugar
3 tablespoons lime juice
½ cup vegetable oil
2 teaspoons chopped garlic
1 block firm tofu (8 to 12 ounces), cut into ½-inch cubes
1 head broccoli, cut into small florets

4 eggs
6 tablespoons chopped roasted unsalted peanuts
1½ cup bean sprouts
3 stalks green onion, cut into 1-inch pieces
1 cup Maui Gold pineapple, julienned
½ teaspoon chopped Thai red chilli (you can substitute Serrano chilli)
6 sprigs cilantro
6 lime wedges

Soak the noodles in cold water for 1–2 hours. The noodles should be completely soft.

Combine the tamarind paste with the warm water in a bowl, and let the mixture soak for at least 30 minutes. After soaking, mash it or pulse it in a food processor. At this point, it should look and feel like thick mud. Transfer the mixture to a strainer set over a bowl. Push the pulp against the strainer with a spatula, forcing the liquid into the bowl. Scrape off the juice that clings to the underside of the strainer and add it to the bowl. You will end up with 6–8 tablespoons of tamarind juice.

Combine the tamarind juice with the fish sauce, sugar, and lime juice. Whisk to mix and set aside. Discard the solids left in the strainer.

Heat the oil in a wok or large frying pan, over high heat, until it begins to smoke slightly or about 1 minute. This lets you know the oil is hot enough for successful stir-frying. Add the garlic and cook for about 30 seconds, stirring constantly. Add the tofu and stir-fry for 1 minute. Add the broccoli and stir-fry for 1 more minute. Break the eggs into the wok or pan and let them fry without breaking them up for 1–2 minutes.

While the eggs cook, quickly drain the noodles and add them to the wok. Give them a quick toss and then stir-fry for 1 minute more while gently tossing the whole mixture, making sure no noodles end up lying on the bottom of the pan, unmixed. Add the reserved tamarind juice and continue stir-frying for 1–2 minutes. Your noodles will have shrunk to ½ their original volume and softened to al dente.

Add about ⅔ of the peanuts and stir. Add about ⅔ of the bean sprouts and all the green onion pieces. Stir-fry for 30 seconds and remove the pad Thai from the heat. Add pineapple and toss to combine.

TO SERVE

Transfer the noodles to a serving dish and sprinkle with chillis. Top with the rest of the peanuts, the rest of the sprouts and the cilantro. Serve with lime wedges on the side.

Grilled Vegetable Crêpes with Goat Cheese

Crêpes are thin unleavened pancakes. They are used in many desserts and savory dishes as wrappers for various tasty fillings. When filling them, put the side of the crêpe that was browned first, the most attractive side, against the counter or cutting board, so that when they are wrapped, the attractive side is on the outside.

The crêpes can be made and stuffed ahead of time. Heat them in a microwave or on a sheet pan in a 325 degree oven before serving. For a lighter crêpe, omit the cheese and reduce the amount of butter. If you do this, you will need to spray the pan with pan-release.

You can easily vary the fillings using different fresh vegetables, fresh herbs and cheeses. Make dessert crêpes with fresh or canned fruits and garnish with sour cream, flavored goat cheese or cottage cheese.

—*Tom Lelli*

CRÊPE FILLING
1 zucchini, cut into ¼-inch slices
1 yellow squash, cut into ¼-inch slices
1 red bell pepper, cut into ¼-inch slices
1 small onion, cut into ¼-inch slices
1 clove garlic, finely chopped
2 tablespoons olive oil
Salt and pepper
2 ounces goat cheese, at room temperature (we like the selection from Maui's Surfing Goat Dairy)
1 (14½ ounce) can green asparagus spears, drained, cut into 1-inch pieces

CRÊPE BATTER
1 cup all-purpose flour
Pinch salt
3 eggs, beaten
1¼ cups dry milk powder, reconstituted according to package directions
2 tablespoons canola oil

Tomato Salsa Fresca (see page 13)

TO PREPARE THE FILLING

Lay the fresh vegetables, including the onion, in a pan with a rim, and brush with olive oil. Season with the garlic, salt, and pepper. Once the vegetables are oiled, you can either grill them on a barbecue (charcoal or gas) or on a griddle or grill pan on your stove. If you don't have access to any of these, you can lightly sauté the vegetables in a pan on the stovetop. When the vegetables are lightly grilled and the onions are soft, remove them from the heat, set them aside, and allow to cool. When cool, chop the grilled vegetables into ¼-inch dice and place them in a mixing bowl. Add the goat cheese and asparagus and mix until evenly distributed. Adjust the seasoning if needed. This filling can be kept in the refrigerator for up to 3 days.

TO PREPARE THE CRÊPES

Place the flour and salt in bowl. In a separate bowl, whisk the eggs and milk together. Then whisk the egg and flour mixtures together. Strain to remove any lumps. Lightly whisk in the oil.

Heat a medium-sized non-stick pan over medium heat for 1 minute. Spray the hot pan with vegetable spray-release and immediately add ¼ cup crepe batter and rotate the pan to evenly distribute the batter. You should hear a slight sizzle in the pan. Cook the crêpe for 30–40 seconds. Flip with a plastic spatula and cook for another 10 seconds.

TO ASSEMBLE THE CRÊPES

You can make all the crêpes at once and stack them with waxed paper in between the crêpes until you are ready to assemble them. To assemble, place 3 tablespoons of filling in the center of the crêpe. Fold over the edges to make a square package like a burrito. If they cool before you are ready to serve them, you will want to heat the folded crêpes in a very lightly oiled sauté pan. You can also warm them up in the microwave for a few seconds

You can also make the crêpes one at a time. When you have finished cooking one crêpe, place 3 tablespoons of filling in the center of the cooked crêpe in the pan. As above, carefully fold over the edges to make a square package like a burrito. Cook for 2 minutes, or until the filling is warm.

TO SERVE

Transfer the warm crêpes to a serving plate and garnish with the tomato salsa fresca.

Lemongrass Coconut Tofu

It's a challenge to create fresh, unique vegetarian dishes. The trick is making a dish that a non-vegetarian would want to eat. I think this recipe accomplishes that.

—*James McDonald*

1 block firm tofu, sliced into ½-inch thick slices and marinated

TOFU MARINADE

1 cup rice wine vinegar
½ cup lime juice
½ cup low-sodium soy sauce
2 tablespoons hoisin sauce
½ cup brown sugar
1 teaspoon Thai chilli paste
1 tablespoon chopped garlic
1 tablespoon chopped shallot
1 tablespoon black and white sesame seeds
½ cup sesame oil

HEARTS OF PALM SALAD

½ cup fresh hearts of palm
½ cup julienned green papaya
½ cup sunflower sprouts
½ cup radish sprouts
¼ cup julienned red beet
¼ cup julienned carrot
2 cups whole leaf herbs (any combination you like—basil, mint, flat parsley, cilantro, chervil)
Salt and pepper to taste

MANGO DRESSING

2 cups mango purée
¼ cup lime juice
¼ cup rice wine vinegar
2 cups canola or other neutral oil
Tabasco to taste
Salt to taste

SWEET BEET VINAIGRETTE

1½ cups peeled and diced red beets
½ cup water
¼ cup sugar
½ cup red wine vinegar
¼ cup balsamic vinegar
1 teaspoons minced shallot
½ vanilla bean, split and scraped; you'll use only the "scrapings" for the vinaigrette
2 cups canola oil
½ cup extra virgin olive oil
Salt and pepper to taste

LEMONGRASS CRUST

1 cup panko (Japanese-style bread crumbs)
1 cup shredded coconut, unsweetened
1 teaspoon black and white sesame seeds
2 teaspoons tahini (sesame paste)
2 teaspoons minced lemongrass
1 teaspoon shichimi spice
1 teaspoon minced kaffir lime leaves

SOBA NOODLES

1 package soba noodles, cooked according to package directions
¼ cup low-sodium soy sauce
2 tablespoons sesame oil
1 teaspoon sambal (chilli paste)
Salt and pepper, to taste

TO MARINATE THE TOFU

Mix all the ingredients for the tofu marinade. Add the tofu to the marinade and marinate overnight, at a minimum. 12 hours is better.

TO PREPARE THE SALAD

Mix all the salad ingredients and chill in the refrigerator.

TO PREPARE THE MANGO DRESSING

Place all ingredients in a blender and blend until well combined. Hold in the refrigerator.

TO PREPARE THE VINAIGRETTE

Place beets, water, and sugar in a saucepot over medium heat and cook until tender, or about 30 minutes. Remove the beets from the heat and chill them in the refrigerator. Place the beet mixture in a blender with the vinegars, oils, shallots, vanilla bean, salt, and pepper; purée the vinaigrette until it is smooth and emulsified. Set aside.

TO SEAR THE TOFU

Assemble the ingredients for the lemongrass crust. Mix the panko, coconut, and sesame seeds together. Spread an even coat of tahini over each tofu slice. Sprinkle with lemongrass, shichimi, and kaffir. Then press the tofu into the coconut mix.

Heat a sauté pan over medium heat and add ¼ cup peanut oil. Place the tofu in the pan and brown on both sides, about two minutes per side. Remove it from the heat.

TO SERVE

Lightly toss the salad with a little mango dressing and seasoning. Place the soba noodles in a bowl with the soy sauce, sesame oil, and sambal, and mix to coat the noodles with sauce. Set out 4–8 salad plates. On each plate, arrange some noodles and then some salad. Place a slice or two of tofu on each salad. Drizzle vinaigrette and mango dressing around each plate and serve.

Serve with the remainder of the vinaigrette and mango dressing on the side. Tip: These sauces can also be stored in the refrigerator for about a week. Use them in salads and as dipping sauces.

Stir-Fried Tofu with Maui Asparagus and Kabocha Squash

SERVES 4–6

Kabocha is a medium to large winter squash that grows amazingly well here on Maui. Its smooth, tender orange flesh and sweet flavor are very appealing.

This healthy recipe is an adaptation from the kitchen of Foodland's Corporate Chef, Keoni Chang. We use Kabocha squash, Maui asparagus, and firm tofu in our recipe. This dish also works wonderfully with shrimp, fish, or chicken.

—Chris Speere

---

2 pounds kabocha squash or pumpkin
3 tablespoons vegetable oil
¼ teaspoon salt
¼ teaspoon pepper
4 tablespoons canola oil
1 tablespoon sesame oil
1 block firm tofu, drained and cut into
  ½ inch cubes
3 tablespoons brown sugar
1 tablespoon grated fresh ginger

1 teaspoon fish sauce
1 clove garlic, chopped
1 pound Maui asparagus or snow peas,
  trimmed
2 tablespoons soy sauce
2 tablespoons oyster sauce
2 tablespoons chopped cilantro
1 teaspoon sambal chilli paste
2 tablespoons sliced green onions

TO PREPARE THE KABOCHA

Preheat the oven to 425 degrees. Peel the squash, cut it in half lengthwise, seed it, and then cut it on the diagonal into 1-inch chunks. Toss the squash with the vegetable oil, salt and pepper. Place the squash in a baking pan and bake in the oven for 30–40 minutes, or until tender.

TO PREPARE THE STIR-FRY

Approximately 5 minutes before squash is cooked tender, add 4 tablespoons canola oil and 1 tablespoon sesame oil to a wok or skillet. Heat oils over medium high heat, then add tofu, brown sugar, ginger, fish sauce, garlic, and asparagus to pan. Stir-fry for 3 minutes or until asparagus is tender.

Remove the kabocha squash from the oven. Add squash to tofu and asparagus. Add the soy sauce, oyster sauce, cilantro and sambal chilli paste, and stir-fry ingredients for 1 more minute. Remove from heat.

TO SERVE

Place the tofu and vegetables on a large platter. Garnish with sliced green onions and serve family-style.

Grilled Jumbo Shrimp
in Maui Gold Pineapple Curry Sauce

SERVES 8

This recipe showcases the exquisite Maui Gold pineapple. The sweetness of the pineapple is the perfect foil to the sharp, spicy flavors of the curry sauce, which is made with red Thai curry paste.

You can adjust the spiciness of this dish by simply adding more or less of the curry paste. The shrimp curry can be served over pasta, brown rice, or steamed kabocha pumpkin.

—Chris Speere

---

2 cups low-sodium chicken broth
1 Maui onion, finely chopped
1 tablespoon red Thai curry paste
1 tablespoon chopped ginger
1 cup diced Maui Gold pineapple
   ($\frac{1}{2}$-inch cubes)
1 can (14-ounce size) unsweetened
   coconut milk
2 tablespoons fish sauce

24 jumbo shrimp, shelled and deveined
2 tablespoons vegetable oil
Salt to taste
1 cup finely diced Maui Gold pineapple
$\frac{1}{2}$ cup shredded coconut, toasted (see
   page 174 for tips)
$\frac{1}{2}$ cup chopped roasted peanuts
$\frac{1}{2}$ cup chopped cilantro

In a large saucepot, combine the chicken stock with the onion, curry paste, ginger, and pineapple. Bring to a boil. Reduce heat to medium and simmer until the mixture is reduced by $\frac{1}{2}$, or about 7 minutes. Stir in the coconut milk and fish sauce and cook until reduced by $\frac{1}{2}$ again, or about 10 minutes more. Remove from heat and strain. Keep hot until ready to serve.

Preheat a barbecue or indoor grill. Brush the shrimp with vegetable oil and season with salt. Grill the shrimp on a hot grill for about 1 minute per side, or until lightly charred and just cooked through.

TO SERVE

Transfer the grilled shrimp to a warm serving platter. Spoon the curry sauce over the shrimp and garnish with the diced pineapple, coconut, peanuts, and cilantro. Serve immediately over rice or noodles.

Crispy Moloka'i Prawns

This is another recipe using one of Maui County's most delicious products: Moloka'i prawns. When used fresh from the sea, these shellfish are sweet, savory, and unsurpassed for flavor and texture. Here the prawns are deep fried with their shells on. This adds a delightful crunch to the finished dish.

Serve on their own or paired with the delicious Taro Cakes on page 43 for a heartier entrée.

—*Chris Speere*

---

18 pieces fresh Moloka'i prawns
1 tablespoon chopped ginger
¼ cup white wine
1 teaspoon + 1 teaspoon salt
½ cup tapioca starch (you may substitute cornstarch)
1 quart peanut oil, for deep frying

½ cup chopped green onions
1 tablespoon minced garlic
½ teaspoon freshly-ground black pepper
¼ cup thinly sliced green onions
Taro cakes (see page 43)

Split the prawns down the back and de-vein. Remove the legs. Combine the ginger, white wine, one teaspoon of the salt, and tapioca starch in a bowl. Add the prawns and marinate for 30 minutes in the refrigerator.

In a large pot, heat the oil to 325 degrees. Fry the shrimp until they are golden brown, or about 2 minutes.

Toss the hot crispy shrimp with the green onions, garlic, and the remaining salt and pepper. To serve with the taro cakes, place 3 shrimp on each taro cake and garnish with green onions. Serve immediately to ensure that the shrimp are really crispy!

Spicy Fresh Shrimp
with Hijiki Tofu Salad

There are many types of tofu in the market place. Be sure to purchase fresh tofu that is sweet and firm. Aburage is readily available in the Japanese section of island grocery stores. You can also add dried shrimp or fishcake to this recipe.

—*Hideo Kurihara*

2 pounds shrimp	**HIJIKI TOFU SALAD**
4 tablespoons chopped green onions	2 tablespoons dry hijiki seaweed
1 tablespoon chopped garlic	1 tablespoon sugar
1 tablespoon chopped ginger	3 tablespoons light soy sauce
1 tablespoon soy sauce	3 pieces aburage (deep-fried tofu)
1 teaspoon Sriracha hot chilli sauce	3 teaspoons canola oil
1 tablespoon sesame oil	1 pound firm tofu
Salt and pepper to taste	

TO PREPARE THE SALAD

Soak the hijiki seaweed in hot water for 10 minutes. Then drain it and squeeze it with your hands to remove all the excess water.

Cut the aburage into thin, 2-inch long shreds. Cut the tofu into 1-inch cubes.

Combine the hijiki tofu salad ingredients in a large mixing bowl. Toss gently. Set aside.

TO PREPARE THE SHRIMP

Peel the shrimp and cut it into $\frac{1}{2}$-inch pieces. Wash it in salted ice water and drain it.

In a medium-size sauté pan, heat the sesame oil over medium heat. Add the shrimp, green onions, garlic, ginger, soy sauce, and chilli sauce. Sauté quickly over high heat for 2 minutes or until the shrimp are partially cooked. Set aside to cool.

TO SERVE

Add shrimp mixture to the hijiki salad and mix well. Add salt and pepper to taste. Serve cold in a large bowl or on a decorative platter.

Moloka'i Sweet Potato Shrimp Cakes

I created this recipe for the Moloka'i Food Expo. I wanted to showcase one of our unique island products, fresh taro, in an easy family-style recipe.

Taro has a brown skin and starchy gray flesh that develops a pleasant nutty flavor when cooked. It is important to cook taro thoroughly, as raw taro can irritate the hands, mouth, and throat. It is best to steam or boil taro in plenty of water.

These shrimp cakes go nicely with the Basil Cream Sauce on page 17. You can also serve the shrimp cakes with poached eggs and classic Hollandaise sauce for a delightful brunch.

—Chris Speere

¾ cup cooked and finely diced purple Moloka'i sweet potato

½ cup cooked and finely diced local taro, cooked

½ cup cooked and chopped Moloka'i shrimp (or any fresh shrimp)

1 tablespoon chopped chives

1 tablespoon chopped cilantro

4 cloves garlic, roasted and chopped

¼ cup finely diced firm tofu

3 tablespoons shredded Parmesan cheese

1 egg

1 teaspoon Moloka'i "Soul of the Sea" Salt, or other coarse salt

½ teaspoon black pepper

½ cup panko flakes (Japanese bread crumbs)

Canola or other neutral oil

Basil Cream Sauce (see page 17)

TO PREPARE THE SHRIMP CAKES

Place all the ingredients for the cakes in a mixing bowl and toss to mix. Lightly mash them with a spoon to make a chunky paste. Divide the mixture into ¼ cup portions. Form them into patties and lightly coat them with panko flakes. Heat a small amount of oil in a skillet over medium heat and pan fry the cakes in the oil for 2 minutes per side, or until they are golden brown.

TO SERVE

Pour ¼ cup of the basil cream sauce on a warm plate and top with a shrimp cake.

Macadamia Nut Prawn Tempura

I created this dish to showcase one of Hawai'i's most famous products: the macadamia nut. Macadamia nuts add a mellow flavor to the tempura, while the warm vinaigrette enhances and harmonizes the flavors of the salad.

—*Darryl Dela Cruz*

---

12 prawns, 16/20 size, peeled and
   deveined
Flour for dredging
½ cup toasted and coarsely chopped
   macadamia nuts (see page 174 for tips)
8 cups mesclun mix (you can substitute
   spring salad mix or baby salad greens)
4 vine-ripened tomatoes, cut into
   quarters
12 wooden skewers
4 cups vegetable oil
4 squares of rice paper, 8 x 8-inch
Warm Macadamia Nut Oil and
   Ginger Vinaigrette (see page 11)

MARINATED ONIONS
¼ cup white vinegar
¼ cup sugar
1 thin-sliced Maui onion

TEMPURA BATTER
¾ cup rice flour
¼ cup cornstarch
1 egg yolk
1 cup ice water
1 teaspoon salt

TO PREPARE THE MARINATED ONIONS

Mix the vinegar and sugar together and stir well, making sure the sugar is completely dissolved. Add the sliced onions and let them marinate for 5–10 minutes.

TO PREPARE THE TEMPURA BATTER

Combine all batter ingredients and mix quickly with whisk, fork, or cooking chopsticks. If there are a few lumps left in the batter, that's fine. Avoid over-mixing. Refrigerate the batter for at least 5 minutes before you dip and fry the shrimp.

TO PREPARE THE RICE PAPER GARNISH

In a large saucepot, heat the vegetable oil to 350 degrees. Soften the rice paper in warm water for about 30 seconds or until pliable. Drain it on paper towels and wipe off the excess water. Cut the rice paper into strips.

When the oil is hot, add the sliced rice paper and cook until crisp and slightly golden, or about 2 minutes. Remove the strips from the oil and drain them on paper towels. Keep the vegetable oil used to fry the rice paper at 350 degrees—you will also use it to deep fry the prawns.

TO PREPARE THE PRAWNS

Skewer each prawn from head to tail to keep it straight when frying. Dredge the shrimp in flour, then dip them into the chilled batter, and then coat them with the chopped macadamia nuts. Deep fry the shrimp until lightly browned, or about 3–4 minutes. Remove and drain on paper towels. Keep warm.

TO ASSEMBLE THE DISH

Stir the vinaigrette well, then toss the greens with ¾ of the dressing. Toss the tomatoes with the remaining vinaigrette. Divide the greens into 4 even portions and place each portion in the center of a serving plate. Place 4 quarters of a tomato in a cross-shaped pattern on top of the greens. Divide the rice paper strips and marinated onions into 4 even portions. Scatter the crispy rice paper strips over the greens on each plate. Remove the skewers from the shrimp and center 3 shrimp on each plate of greens, crisscrossing the tails. Put the marinated onions in the center of the shrimp arrangement. Drizzle any remaining dressing over the dishes. Serve immediately.

Black Pepper Prawns with Mixed Greens

SERVES 6

When I was invited to do a cooking demonstration at the Moloka'i Food Expo, held annually in October, I chose this recipe. It's a delicious showcase for fresh local products. Moloka'i prawns are complemented by our island mangoes and salad greens.

—Dean Louie

30 large Moloka'i prawns, heads on, split down the back

3 cups mixed greens

¾ cup seeded, peeled, and sliced cucumbers

6 cherry tomatoes, halved

6 tablespoons thinly sliced red onion

6 tablespoons julienned carrots

1 purple (Okinawan) sweet potato or Peruvian purple potato, and 1 yellow sweet potato or yam, cooked, cooled, peeled and sliced into rounds, about ½ inch thick

SAUCE

2 tablespoons oyster sauce

1 tablespoon cracked black peppercorns (see tip on page 174)

1 tablespoon diced ginger

1 tablespoon chopped green onion

2 cloves garlic, minced

1 tablespoon neutral oil, like canola

1 tablespoon sherry wine (optional)

Mango Vinaigrette (see page 8)

Combine all ingredients in a bowl and mix well. Set aside.

TO PREPARE THE PRAWNS

Heat a large heavy-duty sauté pan and coat the bottom of the pan with 1 table-spoon of vegetable oil. Add the prawns and sauté for about 2 minutes per side. The prawns are done when they turn pink and opaque.

Add 4 tablespoons water or white wine and 1 tablespoon of sauce. Continue cook-ing until the prawns are coated, glazed, and cooked through.

TO SERVE

Toss the greens with about 1 cup of the vinaigrette. Divide into 6 portions and surround with vegetable and potato garnish. Place 5 of the finished prawns on the salad. Serve with the remainder of the vinaigrette on the side.

Crispy Lobster Cone Sushi

SERVES 4

This recipe was a winner in the 2005 Gohan (rice) in New York recipe contest sponsored by Japan's Department of Agriculture. The contest promoted Japanese heirloom rice. I recruited James, our Raw Fish Camp sushi chef, to help me roll the perfect cone sushi. I love the aromatic flavor and crispness of the fried lobster; I believed it would marry perfectly with the rich and smooth texture of sushi rice. World-renowned chef Mark Miller of the Coyote Café judged the contest and picked our dish! This sushi combines some traditional sushi ingredients (the rice and seaweed) with some novel touches (crunchy deep-fried lobster and a subtle sweet wasabi sauce).

Roll the cone sushi just before serving to keep the nori wrapper crisp. Hot sake is a wonderful accompaniment to this innovative sushi.

—*Chris Speere*

1½ cups diced fresh lobster meat
   (1-inch pieces)
1 quart canola oil

SUSHI
1½ cups sushi rice
1½ cups cold water

LOBSTER MARINADE
3 tablespoons minced ginger (2
   tablespoons for marinade; reserve 1
   tablespoon for lobster seasoning)
3 tablespoons sake
3 tablespoons cornstarch

LOBSTER SEASONING
¼ cup sliced green onions
2 tablespoons minced garlic
Reserved ginger (see above)
1 teaspoon salt
½ teaspoon freshly ground black
   pepper

FOR THE SUSHI ROLL
1 small cucumber, julienned
1 small avocado, sliced
4 sheets temaki yaki nori
Red and black tobiko (optional)

Sweet Wasabi Sauce (see page 19)

TO PREPARE THE SUSHI RICE

Cook and cool the sushi rice as follows: thoroughly rinse the rice until the water runs clear, approximately 3 minutes. Drain the rice in a colander for 10 minutes. Put the rice into an electric rice cooker with the pre-measured water and cook the rice. Once the rice is done, let it stand covered for 10 minutes. After 10 minutes, turn the rice out into a shallow medium-size wooden or plastic bowl. Cool the rice by using a rice paddle or plastic spatula to cut horizontally through the cooked rice, over and over again. Periodically dip your rice paddle into cold water to keep the rice from sticking to the paddle. By exposing all the rice to the cool air, you are

(recipe continued on page 100)

cooling it quickly and uniformly. Continue cutting until the rice is completely cool; this should take approximately 10–15 minutes.

TO PREPARE THE LOBSTER

Marinate the lobster meat in the ginger, sake and cornstarch. Refrigerate for 15 minutes. Deep fry the lobster in a large saucepot in 350 degree canola oil until crispy and golden brown, or approximately 3 minutes. Remove the lobster from the hot oil and put in a medium-size bowl. Toss and season the lobster with the sliced green onions, reserved minced garlic, salt and pepper. Set aside.

TO SERVE

Cut each temaki yaki nori sheet in half to make 8 pieces. Place ¼ cup cooked sushi rice on top of 1 nori sheet. Top the rice with 3–4 pieces of the deep-fried seasoned lobster followed by 3 pieces of julienned cucumber, 2 slices of avocado, and 1 teaspoon of the sweet wasabi sauce. If desired, add 1 teaspoon each of the red and black tobiko. Roll the sushi into a cone shape and serve immediately. Repeat the process to make a total of 8 uniform cone sushi.

Crab Cakes with Papaya Beurre Blanc and Tropical Salsa

SERVES 6

These crab cakes easy to make and, if I do say so myself, delicious! The beurre blanc sauce and the colorful salsa add a slightly sweet touch to this wonderful dish.

—*Elaine Rothermel*

1½ pounds crabmeat, shredded
2 stalks lemongrass, white part only, minced
2 tablespoons minced ginger
2 tablespoons minced garlic
½ teaspoon red pepper flakes
½ cup sliced green onions
¼ cup chopped cilantro
1 cup panko (Japanese bread crumbs)
1 tablespoon black sesame seeds
1 tablespoon white sesame seeds
1 cup mayonnaise
2 tablespoons sweet Thai chilli sauce
1 egg
Salt and pepper to taste
Olive oil for sautéing
¼ cup shredded Napa cabbage

PAPAYA BEURRE BLANC
1 tablespoon chopped garlic
1 teaspoon black peppercorns

½ medium papaya, diced (approximately 1 cup)
1 bay leaf
¾ cup white wine
½ cup heavy cream
½ pound unsalted butter, cut into small pieces
Juice of ½ lemon
Salt and pepper to taste

TROPICAL SALSA
½ medium papaya, finely diced (approximately 1 cup)
2 tablespoons finely diced pineapple
1 teaspoon finely chopped cilantro
1 teaspoon finely diced red bell pepper
1 teaspoon finely diced red onion
2 teaspoons lemon juice
Salt and pepper to taste

TO PREPARE THE CRAB CAKES

Combine all the ingredients in a bowl and mix well. Shape the mixture into 12 patties and sauté them in olive oil over medium heat until golden brown, about 3–4 minutes per side. Immediately put the crab cakes on a baking sheet and finish cooking them in a preheated 375 degree oven for 6–8 minutes. The cakes should be hot on the inside, while remaining golden brown on the outside.

TO PREPARE THE PAPAYA BEURRE BLANC

In a small saucepan, sauté the garlic, black peppercorns, papaya, bay leaf ,and white wine over medium heat. Simmer until the liquid is reduced by ½. Add the

(recipe continued on page 102)

cream and reduce again by ⅓. Slowly whisk the pieces of butter into the sauce, whisking until the sauce is smooth. Strain the sauce through a chinois. If you don't have a chinois, a fine strainer will work well. Add the lemon juice. Season with salt and pepper. Keep warm until ready to serve.

TO PREPARE THE SALSA

Combine all the ingredients in a medium-size bowl and season to taste.

TO SERVE

Put a "bed" of napa cabbage on each plate. Place 2 crab cakes per plate on top of the Napa cabbage and then ladle 3 tablespoons of sauce over them. Top with salsa. Serve.

Dungeness Crab Cakes with Three Bell Peppers, Sweet Curry Coconut Cream, and Bean Threads

SERVES 4–6

This dish is influenced by southern Thai and Malaysian cuisine. Curry and creamy coconut milk are a tasty and aromatic pair; they also add great color to the dish. The crabmeat and bell peppers accent and harmonize.

—*Suwanlee Pease*

1 pound Dungeness crab meat (brown and white meat)	**SAUCE**
¼ cup finely diced red bell pepper	¼ teaspoon vegetable oil
¼ cup finely diced green bell pepper	1 tablespoon finely chopped shallots
¼ cup finely diced yellow bell pepper	1 can (13½-ounce size) coconut milk
2 tablespoons chopped fresh garlic chives	2 tablespoons curry powder
3 tablespoons mayonnaise	1½ teaspoons salt
1½ cups cornbread crumbs	1 tablespoon sugar
Neutral oil	½ teaspoon freshly ground black pepper
1 package bean threads (2 ounce size)	
2 tablespoons finely chopped cilantro leaves	**CORNSTARCH SLURRY**
	2 tablespoons cornstarch
	4 tablespoons cold water

TO PREPARE THE CRAB CAKES

Mix the crab meat, three kinds of bell peppers, chives, and mayonnaise in a bowl. Stir in the cornbread crumbs to make a mixture that is firm enough to form patties but is not too stiff. Form the mixture into 12 cakes. Cover and then chill the cakes for 30 minutes. Heat a shallow layer of oil in a frying pan over medium heat. Fry the crab cakes until they are golden brown, or about 3–4 minutes per side.

TO PREPARE THE SAUCE

Mix the cornstarch and cold water to form a slurry, making sure that there are no lumps (see page 176 for tips). Set aside.

In a medium-size saucepot over medium heat, sauté the shallots in the vegetable oil until they are soft, or about 2 minutes. Add the coconut milk and curry powder; hold the sauce at a slow boil for about 5 minutes. Season with salt, sugar, and ground black pepper. Thicken the sauce with the cornstarch and water slurry. Keep the sauce warm until you are ready to serve the dish.

TO PREPARE THE GARNISH

Deep fry the noodles according to package directions. If you are not going to use them immediately, they can be stored in an air tight container until you are ready to serve.

TO SERVE

Spoon a dollop of sauce onto each of 4–6 plates. Place the deep-fried bean threads in the center of the pool of sauce. Arrange 2 crab cakes on top of the bean threads. Sprinkle with chopped cilantro leaves. Serve with the remaining sauce on the side.

Furikake-Seared Scallops with Kim Chee Cream

SERVES 4

Furikake-seared fish used to be novel; now it's old hat. I wanted to give the dish a new twist and after some experimentation, came up with this sauce. It is simple, tasty and, for me, nothing goes better with furikake than kim chee!

The recipe calls for kim chee base, which you can buy in the Asian food section of most island supermarkets.

—*Lyndon Honda*

20 scallops, 10/20 count
6 tablespoons furikake
¼ cup peanut oil

CORNSTARCH SLURRY
1 tablespoon cornstarch mixed with
   2–3 tablespoons of cold water

KIM CHEE CREAM
1½ teaspoons sesame oil
1 shallot, finely diced
½ cup white wine
1½ tablespoons kim chee base
1 cup heavy whipping cream
4 tablespoons (½ stick) unsalted
   butter

CUCUMBER KIM CHEE
1 cup seeded and julienned cucumber
3-4 tablespoons kim chee base

TO PREPARE THE CUCUMBER KIM CHEE

Mix the cucumbers with the kim chee base and let stand for about 30 minutes. Mix again before serving.

TO PREPARE THE KIM CHEE CREAM

In a saucepot over medium heat, heat the sesame oil and sauté the shallots and kim chee base until the shallots are translucent, or about 2 minutes. To deglaze, add the white wine to the pan and stir to dissolve any crusts on the pan bottom. To reduce the liquid, cook at low heat until the liquid is almost completely evaporated. This should take no more than 1 minute.

Add the cream and bring to a boil. Mix the cornstarch and cold water to form a slurry (see page 176 for tips). Slowly whisk the cornstarch slurry into the cream and simmer for about 15 minutes, until the sauce is the consistency of heavy syrup. Gradually whisk the butter into the sauce until it is thoroughly mixed. Remove from direct heat and keep warm on top of the stove or in a hot water bath.

TO PREPARE THE SCALLOPS

Press one side of each scallop into the furikake to form a crust. In a sauté pan over medium heat, heat the peanut oil until it just begins to smoke, or about 1 minute. Sear each side of each scallop for approximately 1 minute. Be sure not to overcook the scallops; if you do, they will be rubbery.

TO SERVE

Ladle 2 tablespoons of the kim chee cream on each plate and place 5 furikake-seared scallops on the cream. Place a spoonful of cucumber kim chee on the side.

SEAFOOD · SALMON

Pan-Seared Salmon with Red Wine Beluga Lentils

SERVES 4

I love lentils, especially black beluga lentils. Cooked with red wine, these lentils develop a hearty taste that complements the luscious pan-seared salmon. Velvety Smooth Yukon Gold Potato and Parsnip Purée is the perfect accompaniment (see recipe on page 81).

—*Tom Lelli*

LENTILS
1 tablespoon neutral oil, like canola
2 pieces bacon, finely diced
$\frac{1}{2}$ cup finely chopped onion
1 clove minced garlic
$\frac{1}{2}$ cup finely diced carrots
$\frac{1}{4}$ cup finely diced celery
$\frac{1}{4}$ cup finely diced leek, white part only (be sure to wash well; leeks are often sandy)
2 sprigs fresh thyme, chopped
$2\frac{1}{2}$ cups full-bodied red wine (the Plantation Red from Maui's Tedeschi Winery works well here)
1 cup beluga lentils (or you can substitute French green lentils)

1 bay leaf
1 cinnamon stick
4 cups chicken or vegetable stock
Salt and fresh ground pepper to taste

SALMON
4 salmon filets, (approximately 6 ounces each)
2–3 tablespoons neutral oil, like canola
Salt and fresh ground pepper to taste

Crème fraîche (see recipe on page 24)
Red tobiko (optional)
1 lemon, thinly sliced (optional)

(recipe continued on page 107)

Heat a saucepot over medium heat. Add the oil and bacon and sauté the bacon until the bacon fat is rendered (melted out of the bacon meat), which should take about 3–4 minutes. Add the onion, garlic, carrot, celery, leeks, and thyme, cover the pan, lower the heat slightly, and sweat the bacon and vegetables for 5 minutes. (See page 177 for tips on sweating food.) Turn the contents of the pan into a bowl and put the pan back on the heat; add the wine. Stir to deglaze the pan, so that the bacon and vegetable fats and juices mingle with the wine. Boil the seasoned wine until it is reduced by half. Pour off the wine and reserve.

TO PREPARE THE LENTILS

Add the lentils, stock, cooked vegetables and bacon to a medium saucepot and simmer until the lentils start to become tender. This may take about 25 minutes. Add the reduced wine sauce at this point. You may wish to add it a little at a time, stopping when you feel that the flavor is just right. Season with salt and pepper to taste and simmer approximately 10 minutes more.

TO PREPARE THE SALMON

Season the salmon with salt and pepper on both sides. Heat a large sauté pan or skillet over high heat and add oil. When the oil is very hot but not smoking place salmon carefully in the pan and cook until brown, or about 2 minutes. Turn the salmon over and cook another 1–2 minutes (longer if you like your fish well-done).

Note: The salmon in this photo was done with a classic French technique called a roulade, where essentially, the salmon filet is butterflied, seasoned and rolled up. It is then seared on each end then finished in the oven. This is great for an excellent presentation, but you can also prepare this dish simply, as noted above, without doing a roulade.

TO SERVE

If using, place a serving of the Velvety Smooth Yukon Gold Potato and Parsnip Puree in the center of 4 plates. Arrange the lentils around the potato puree. Place a salmon fillet on top of the puree. Garnish with crème fraîche (see recipe on page 24), red tobiko, and lemon, if desired.

Honey-Baked Salmon with Ginger Fruit Relish

This recipe was created for a heart-healthy cooking contest sponsored by HMSA, the Hawai'i Medical Services Association. It won first place and was the dish served at the HMSA booth at the Taste of Honolulu culinary festival several years ago.

—*Elaine Rothermel*

4 salmon fillets (approximately 6 ounces each)
2 tablespoons Dijon mustard
1 tablespoon ground ginger
1 tablespoon honey
⅛ teaspoon black pepper
Vegetable pan-release spray

GINGER FRUIT RELISH
2 cups finely diced mango
1 cup finely diced pineapple

¼ cup finely diced Maui onion
½ cup finely diced cucumber
1 tablespoon finely diced red bell pepper
2 tablespoons finely chopped parsley
3 teaspoons cider vinegar
4 tablespoons lemon juice
2 tablespoons minced ginger
1 tablespoon honey
1 teaspoon olive oil

TO PREPARE THE SALMON

Preheat the oven to 325 degrees. Combine the mustard, ginger powder, honey, and pepper in a small bowl. Spray an ovenproof sauté pan with pan-release and place the salmon fillets in the pan. Brush the fillets with the honey mixture. Cook at high heat on the stove for 2 minutes, then remove the pan from the heat and turn the salmon over. Place the pan in the preheated oven and cook until the salmon is done, or about 6–8 minutes.

TO PREPARE THE FRUIT RELISH

Combine all ingredients in a bowl and mix well. Refrigerate until ready to serve.

TO SERVE

Place each salmon fillet on a plate and top with a spoonful of fruit relish. Serve immediately, with the remaining fruit relish on the side.

Island Catch with Citrus Brown Butter

SERVES 4

The first time I tasted Trout Grenoblaise (made with brown butter, lemon segments, capers, and parsley) at culinary school, I said to myself "Now, this is how fish should taste!" The nutty flavor and aroma of the brown butter are a perfect complement to the lemon and salty capers. Every time I show my new students how to make brown butter, initial frowns of doubt are replaced by smiles of delight. Who could have imagined that burning butter could make it taste so good?

Mahimahi, ono, or any white snapper is an excellent choice for this quick and easy preparation.

—*Tom Lelli*

4 white fish fillets (6–7 ounces each), cut $\frac{1}{2}$ to $\frac{3}{4}$-inch thick
Flour for dredging
$\frac{1}{2}$ cup canola oil
Salt and fresh ground pepper to taste

CITRUS BROWN BUTTER
8 tablespoons (1 stick) cold butter, cut into $\frac{1}{2}$-inch pieces
1 orange, cut into segments
1 grapefruit, cut into segments
1 lemon, cut into segments
Juice of 1 lemon
1 tablespoon chopped parsley

Season the fish fillets with salt and pepper. Dredge each fillet in flour and shake off the excess.

Preheat a large sauté pan or two smaller ones over medium heat. Add the canola oil to the pan(s) and let the oil get hot. The oil will shimmer and look like water when the temperature is right. If the oil smokes, the pan is too hot. Using a pair of tongs, carefully lay each fish fillet into the oil. Lay the end that hits the pan first closest you and drop the other end away from you so you do not splash hot oil onto your hand. Sauté the fish for 2–3 minutes on each side until it has a nice golden brown crust. Remove the fish to the serving plates.

Pour the excess oil from the pan and return the pan to high heat. When the pan is hot, add the cold butter pieces. The pan should be hot enough that the butter immediately starts to turn brown. Once all the butter is brown, add the citrus segments, lemon juice, and parsley, and season with salt and pepper. Cook for about 15–30 seconds to reduce the liquid. It reduces quickly, so a short time is enough.

Pour the citrus brown butter over fish and serve.

Pan-Seared ʻŌpakapaka

Any fresh island fish can be used in this recipe. Moi is a great choice. This delicious fish was once reserved for Hawaiian royalty; now it is raised by several local aquaculture companies and is more widely available. Whichever fish you choose, slightly undercook it so that it remains moist and tender.

I like to serve this dish with two different sauces: a Ginger Beurre Blanc Sauce (see page 17) and a Sweet Soy Syrup (see page 19). The Maui Corn Relish (see page 16) is also a wonderful side for this dish. Of course, you can also enjoy the ʻōpakapaka on its own or with your favorite accompaniments.

—Chris Speere

---

6 ʻŌpakapaka fillets (approximately 3-ounce portions), cut on the bias with the skin left on
3 tablespoons canola oil
2 tablespoons butter
½ cup sliced green onions
6 sprigs cilantro

Ginger Beurre Blanc Sauce (see page 17)
Sweet Soy Syrup (see page 19)
Maui Corn Relish (see page 16)

TO PREPARE THE FISH

With a sharp knife, score the ʻŌpakapaka skin, making diagonal score marks about 2 inches apart. Be very careful not to cut into the flesh. Season both sides of the fillets with salt and pepper.

In a large sauté pan, heat the canola oil and butter on medium heat. Cook for 1 minute or so. The butter should be melted and lightly browned. Place the fish skin side down in the sauté pan. Cook until the skin is crispy (approximately 1 minute). Turn the fish over and cook until the fillets are close to completely cooked (another minute or so). The fish will continue cooking even after you remove it from the heat, so be careful not to overcook.

TO ASSEMBLE

Set out 6 plates and place a spoonful of the Maui Corn Relish (see page 16) in the center of each plate. Put one fillet on each plate, on the relish, skin side down. Drizzle about 4 tablespoons of the Ginger Beurre Blanc Sauce around the fish; add some Sweet Soy Syrup in the same fashion. To round out the presentation and to further bring out the Asian-style flavors of the dish, serve with sushi and pickled ginger. Garnish with green onions and cilantro sprigs.

Island Fish with Pecans, Southern-Style

SERVES 4

In the southern United States, this recipe is made with catfish. In the islands, we can use tilapia, 'ōpakapaka, or onaga. It's simple enough that I can make it the way I like it best: cooked over an open fire at my campsite.

This dish is best served with tartar sauce. It works well with side dishes like coleslaw or brown rice and beans.

—*Craig Granger*

4 fish fillets (approximately 6 to 8 ounces each)
3 to 5 tablespoons oil
2½ tablespoons lemon juice (the juice from one medium-size lemon)
½ cup mayonnaise

BREADING
½ cup finely ground corn meal
1 cup lightly toasted and finely chopped pecans (see page 174 for tips)
1 teaspoon cayenne pepper or red chilli flakes for color and heat
½ teaspoon paprika

(recipe continued on page 112)

TO PREPARE THE BREADING

Thoroughly mix the corn meal, chopped pecans, pepper, and paprika. Taste the breading. Is it hot enough for you? Add more cayenne pepper if you'd like more heat.

TO PREPARE THE FISH

Season the fish with salt and pepper prior to coating. Toss the fillets in the lemon juice, then coat liberally with the mayonnaise. Scrape the excess mayonnaise off the fish and place the fish in the breading mixture. Be sure to press the mixture onto the fish firmly so that it stays on the fillet.

Put the oil in a sauté pan over medium-high heat. Pan-fry the fillets immediately after breading them; otherwise, the breading may flake or fall off. Cook for 3–5 minutes on each side, until the breading is golden brown and the fish breaks apart easily.

Pan-Seared Hawaiian Onaga with Local Vegetable Hot Pot and Miso Broth

SERVES 6

I think this is the perfect pairing for onaga. The light, earthy miso broth and root vegetables make a divine, if subtle, background for the snapper. Each vegetable, from the mushrooms to the eggplant, adds a unique texture and flavor to add to the dish.

If you can't find Honshimeji mushrooms, you can substitute other mushroom varieties. I would recommend chanterelles if they are available. However, any forest mushroom will nicely compliment the broth.

—John Cox

6 onaga fillets (approximately 5 ounces each), skin on, sliced on the bias
¼ cup canola oil
1 teaspoon sesame oil
2 cups peeled and sliced Japanese eggplant
1 cup sliced daikon (use a small root rather than a large, coarse one)
1 cup sliced baby carrots
2 cups Honshimeji mushrooms, washed well and broken into clusters of 4–5 mushrooms

2 cups sliced baby bok choy
(Note that all the vegetables should be sliced into bite-size pieces)
2 cups barley
½ cup finely sliced chives
1 cup watercress leaves

MISO BROTH
2 quarts water
1 sheet kombu seaweed
1 pinch bonito flakes
3 tablespoons Hawaiian red miso

In a large saucepot, bring the water to a simmer and add the kombu and bonito flakes. Turn off the heat and let the seaweed and bonito steep as if making a tea. After approximately 10 minutes, or once you reach the desired intensity, strain the "tea" into another large saucepot and discard the solids. Keep the broth at a simmer and just before serving, stir in the red miso to taste.

Lightly toast the barley in a dry, hot sauté pan over medium heat for 1–2 minutes, or until you start to smell the rich barley aroma. Put 2 cups of the miso broth in a saucepot, add the barley, and cook over low heat until the barley is soft. This should take about 4–6 minutes. This process is much like cooking oatmeal.

In another saucepot, poach the vegetables in the remaining miso broth until they are tender, or about 2 minutes.

TO PREPARE THE FISH

Heat the canola and sesame oil in a large sauté pan over high heat for about 1 minute, until the oil begins to smoke. Reduce the heat to medium and sauté the fish, skin side down, over medium heat until the sides of the fillets begin to curl, or approximately 1–2 minutes. Turn the fish over and cook an additional minute or until the fillets are medium-rare. Remove the fillets from the sauté pan and keep them warm until you are ready to serve.

TO SERVE

Divide the poached vegetables and the cooked barley equally between 6 large bowls. Place the fish, skin side up, on top of the vegetables. Pour the hot miso broth over the vegetables just before serving. Garnish with the sliced chives and watercress leaves.

Soused Opah with Yogurt Sauce

SERVES 6

I entered this recipe in the 1991 Second Annual Seafood Festival Competition, held at Honolulu's 'Ilikai Nikko Hotel, and it won! Moloka'i Sweet Potato Cakes (see page 44) go perfectly with the soused opah.

—*James McDonald*

1 opah fillet (approximately 12 ounces), skin and bones removed
1 to 1½ tablespoons fresh lemon juice
1 to 1½ tablespoons fresh lime juice
1 tablespoon canola oil
1 tablespoon sake
1 tablespoon mirin (rice wine)
1 tablespoon soy sauce
2 tablespoons kosher salt
2 tablespoons sugar
2 tablespoons white peppercorns, crushed
2 tablespoons chopped cilantro
Moloka'i Sweet Potato Cakes (see page 44)

2 tablespoons sliced green onions
2 tablespoons chopped fresh cilantro
2 tablespoons tobiko caviar

YOGURT SAUCE
½ cup plain yogurt
½ cup sour cream
1 teaspoon rice wine vinegar
1 tablespoon finely chopped green onion
½ teaspoon sweet yellow mustard
¼ teaspoon salt
¼ teaspoon pepper

TO PREPARE THE OPAH

In a small bowl combine the lemon juice, lime juice, oil, sake, mirin and soy sauce. Coat the fillet with this mixture.

In another small bowl mix together the salt, sugar, crushed white peppercorns, and cilantro and press this mixture onto the meat side of the fillet.

Lay the fillet skin side up in a small pan, cover, and refrigerate for two days, turning the fish every 12 hours to ensure that both sides are equally marinated.

Remove the fish from marinade, wipe it dry with an absorbent towel, and cut it as thinly as possible into 24 uniform slices. Set aside in refrigerator until it is time to assemble the dish.

TO PREPARE THE YOGURT SAUCE

Combine all the ingredients in a small bowl and refrigerate.

TO SERVE

Place a warm sweet potato cake in the center of each plate. Surround each cake with 3-4 thin slices of the soused opah. Drizzle 1 tablespoon of the yogurt sauce over each cake and garnish with tobiko caviar, and, if desired, with sliced green onions and chopped cilantro.

"MediterrAsian" Mahimahi

I had originally planned a dish that would combine the cuisines of two distinct regions, the Mediterranean and Asia. After much experimentation, the final preparation ended up being representative not only those two regions but of India and the Middle East as well. Impossible? Try it and see!

You can use almost any fish for this dish: snapper, ulua, sea bass, monchong, opah…all of these work well. If you prefer grilled fish, you can prepare it in a grill pan on your stovetop or on your barbecue grill.

—*Lyndon Honda*

---

8 pieces of mahimahi (approximately 2 $\frac{1}{2}$ ounces each)
$\frac{1}{4}$ cup olive oil for sautéing the fish (this need not be extra virgin)
1 cup cooked white rice, kept warm

MARINADE FOR MAHIMAHI
1 cup extra virgin olive oil
2 teaspoons turmeric powder
2 teaspoons curry powder
$\frac{1}{4}$ cup finely sliced basil (cut in a chiffonade; see page 175 for tips)
2 teaspoons Hawaiian salt
1 teaspoon black pepper
Juice of 1 lemon

POMODORO SAUCE
2 large tomatoes, finely diced; or 2 cups tomato concasse

$\frac{1}{2}$ cup chopped Maui onion
2-3 tablespoons finely sliced basil (cut in a chiffonade; see page 175 for tips)
$\frac{1}{4}$ teaspoon extra virgin olive oil
Juice of $\frac{1}{4}$ lemon
$\frac{1}{4}$ teaspoon Hawaiian salt
$\frac{1}{4}$ teaspoon black pepper

SAUTÉED SPINACH
2 cups raw spinach, well washed
1 tablespoon olive oil
Hawaiian salt and black pepper

MEDITERRANEAN GARNISHES
$\frac{1}{4}$ cup chopped flat leaf parsley
$\frac{1}{4}$ cup grated Parmesan cheese
$\frac{1}{4}$ cup minced mixed green olives
$\frac{1}{4}$ cup crumbled feta cheese

TO MARINATE THE FISH

Combine the 2 cups of extra virgin olive oil, the turmeric, curry, basil, and salt, and mix well. Reserve $\frac{3}{4}$ cup of this marinade mixture for later use.

Put the fish in the remainder of the mixture and marinate covered for 3-4 hours in the refrigerator.

TO MAKE THE POMODORO SAUCE

A tomato concasse contains tomatoes that have been peeled, seeded, and chopped. To make this, follow the directions for How to Peel Tomatoes on page 175. Once you have the 2 tomatoes peeled, cut them into 6 wedges and then remove the seeds. You should be left with just a thin layer of tomato "meat." Cut this into a small dice. (You can also just dice the 2 tomatoes without peeling or seeding them). Put all the ingredients in a medium-size bowl and mix well. Hold the sauce at room temperature until it is time to serve the fish.

TO PREPARE THE SPINACH

Pour the olive oil into a small sauté pan over high heat. Cook the spinach very quickly, for about 30 seconds or until it starts to wilt. Remove the pan from the heat, season the spinach with the salt and pepper, and hold the spinach until you are ready to serve the fish.

TO HEAT THE MARINADE

Place the ¾ cup of reserved marinade into a small saucepot over low heat. Bring the marinade to a simmer. Remove from heat and keep warm until it is time to serve the fish.

TO COOK THE FISH

Remove the fish from the marinade and allow it to drain. Pour ¼ cup olive oil into a sauté pan and heat for approximately 1 minute, or until the oil just starts to smoke. Sauté the fish for 2 minutes on each side. Remove the fish from the pan and keep it warm in a 250 degree oven.

TO ASSEMBLE THE DISH

Put ¼ cup of cooked rice into the center of each plate. Top the rice with sautéed spinach. Place 2 pieces of fish on top of the spinach and spoon the Pomodoro Sauce on top of the fish. Finish each plate with a drizzle of the reserved marinade and a sprinkling of the Mediterranean garnishes.

Island-Style Fish and Chips

This is a local twist on a much-loved classic. We use Japanese rice flour in the batter and Maui's own taro and sweet potatoes for the chips. Serve the fish with the traditional malt vinegar or your favorite tartar sauce. Or better yet— try my favorite accompaniment, Caper Lemon Relish Sauce (see page 20).

Any white firm fish works well in this dish. Try snapper, halibut, or mahimahi. I suggest mixing the batter—any frying batter for that matter—with your hands. It's the only way you can feel the true texture of your mix. As for getting the slices of taro and sweet potato thin enough to make the chips, a mandolin works well. Most food processors have a shredder attachment that will work for this, too. If you don't have access to either of those methods, slice them as thinly as you can with a very sharp knife, being very careful, of course! For more tips on deep frying, see page 177.

—Darryl Dela Cruz

---

12 firm white fish fillets (approximately 2 ounces each)
Salt and black pepper to taste
1¼ cups milk
3 tablespoons fresh lemon juice
1¼ cups rice flour
1 cup cornstarch
2 teaspoons baking powder
1¼ tablespoons salt
2 tablespoons sugar
1 egg

1 cup ice water
Flour for dredging
2 quarts vegetable or canola oil
Caper Lemon Relish Sauce (see page 20)

SWEET POTATO AND TARO CHIPS
1 cup thinly sliced raw taro
1 cup thinly sliced raw sweet potato
1½ quarts oil
Salt

TO PREPARE THE FISH
Season the fish fillets with salt and pepper. Set aside while making the batter.

TO PREPARE THE BATTER
In a small mixing bowl, combine the milk and lemon juice and let the mixture stand until it is slightly thickened and looks textured instead of smooth; this should take about 5 minutes.

In a separate bowl, sift together the flour, cornstarch, baking powder, salt, and sugar. Add the milk mixture, the eggs, and the ice water. Blend well with a whisk, or better yet, with your hands. The batter should be slightly lumpy. It must be kept cold; put it in the refrigerator if you aren't going to use it immediately.

TO MAKE THE CHIPS

In a medium-sized fry pan, heat the oil over medium heat to 300 degrees (use a frying thermometer to gauge the heat). Fry the taro and sweet potato chips until they are crisp, or about 3–4 minutes. Drain the chips on paper towels and season them with salt.

TO COMPLETE THE DISH

Heat the 2 quarts of canola oil in a large pot to 350 degrees. Dust the fish fillets in flour, then dip them into the batter. Let any excess batter drip off. Fry the fish fillets in the hot oil until they are golden and crisp, or about 1 minute per side. Serve with the sweet potato and taro chips, and the caper lemon relish sauce on the side.

Coconut Macadamia Nut Crusted Catch with Thai Peanut Coconut Sauce, Sweet & Sour Glaze, and Tropical Fruit Salsa

SERVES 4

This is one of my signature dishes. It was created to showcase Hawai'i Regional Cuisine with all its tropical and fusion subtleties. It has remained on my menu at Pacific'O for twelve years and is the number-one-selling dish to this day. Any snapper or mahimahi works well in this recipe.

—James McDonald

4 fresh fish fillets (approximately 5 ounces each)
Peanut oil

THAI PEANUT COCONUT SAUCE
1 tablespoon chopped lemongrass (chopped semi-fine)
1 tablespoon roughly chopped ginger
1 tablespoon roughly chopped garlic
¼ cup lime juice
¼ cup sake
1 cup chicken stock
1 cup coconut milk
2 cups peanut butter
1 teaspoon sambal chilli paste (approximate; you can adjust this amount to your preferred "hotness")
Salt to taste

SWEET & SOUR GLAZE
1 cup sugar
2 teaspoons cinnamon powder
¼ cup red wine vinegar

¼ cup white wine vinegar
2 tablespoons low sodium soy sauce
2 cups rice wine vinegar
2 teaspoons red chilli flakes
2 cinnamon sticks

TROPICAL FRUIT SALSA
½ cup diced pineapple
½ cup diced papaya
½ cup diced mango
¼ cup finely diced onion
2 tablespoons roughly chopped cilantro

CRUST
1 cup chopped macadamia nuts (chopped semi-fine)
½ cup unsweetened shredded coconut
¼ cup panko (Japanese bread crumbs)
½ cup flour
3 eggs, beaten
Salt and pepper to taste

TO PREPARE THE SAUCE

In a saucepot over medium heat, dry sauté the lemongrass, ginger and garlic for 1 minute. Add the lime juice and sake. Cook until the volume is reduced by ½. Add the chicken stock and reduce by ½ again. Add the coconut milk and peanut butter and let the sauce simmer for 15 minutes. Strain, add the sambal, and salt to taste.

TO PREPARE THE SALSA

Combine all ingredients and refrigerate until time to serve.

TO PREPARE THE GLAZE

Place all the glaze ingredients into a saucepot over medium heat. Bring to a boil; then immediately turn the heat to low. Simmer for 20 minutes, stirring occasionally. Remove the cinnamon sticks before serving.

TO PREPARE THE FISH

Assemble the ingredients for the crust. Mix the chopped macadamia nuts, coconut, and panko together in a shallow pan. Put the flour in a separate shallow pan and the eggs in yet another. Set up a breading station by placing the pans in a row. Dip the fish fillets in the flour, then in the eggs, and then in the nut mixture. Bread only *one* side of the fish. Set the fish on a plate or wire rack while you prepare the sauté pan.

Add peanut oil to a sauté pan over medium heat. Season the fish with salt and pepper and place in the sauté pan, nut-side down, and cook until golden brown, or approximately 4 minutes. Turn the fish over and sauté for another 4 minutes. Remove the fish from the heat and set aside, covered, until ready to serve.

TO SERVE

Ladle a little Thai peanut coconut sauce onto the middle of each plate. Place a piece of fish in the center of the sauce. Spoon a little sweet & sour glaze over the top of the fish. Top that with tropical fruit salsa.

Pan-Seared Mahimahi with Herb Crust

Fresh mahimahi takes wonderfully to the flavors of Latin America. If you prefer a touch of "heat," add 1 teaspoon chilli powder and ½ teaspoon cayenne pepper to the herb crust. Toasting the spices just before use refreshes and enlivens the spices' original flavors (see page 174 for tips).

This herb-crusted fish goes perfectly with the avocado butter topping on page 23.

—Bob Cambra

---

24 ounces (1½ pounds) fresh mahimahi fillet
½ cup mayonnaise
Avocado Butter (see page 23)

HERB CRUST
2 tablespoons cumin seeds, toasted
2 cups panko (Japanese-style bread crumbs)
½ cup cornmeal
¼ cup chopped basil

TO PREPARE THE HERB CRUST

In a coffee or spice grinder, grind the cumin seeds into a coarse powder. In a large bowl, mix the ground cumin seed with the panko, cornmeal, and basil.

TO PREPARE THE FISH

Cut the mahimahi into 6 portions, each approximately 4 ounces. Season with salt and pepper. Coat the fish with mayonnaise and then roll it in the herb crust mixture.

Heat 6 tablespoons of vegetable oil in a sauté pan over medium heat. Add the mahimahi and sauté until the fish is thoroughly cooked and the crust is nicely browned, or approximately 3 minutes on each side.

TO ASSEMBLE THE DISH

Set out 6 plates and place one mahimahi piece on each dish. Garnish with a dollop of avocado butter.

Pacific Mussels with Portuguese Sausage

SERVES 4

This dish comes from my home kitchen. A friend brought a box of mussels to a backyard barbecue and suggested that I do something "new" with them. This recipe is the result. It is truly easy to prepare.

Although this dish was originally a family-style pūpū, you could serve it over a thin pasta, like angel hair, as an entrée. Whether you're serving it as a pūpū or an entrée, be sure to accompany it with some fresh bread for dipping!

—*Randi Cua*

---

2 tablespoons olive oil
1/2 cup diced Maui onion
1 1/2 cups sliced Portuguese sausage
   (homemade or store-bought)
4 cloves garlic, sliced
20 mussels on half shell (found in the
   frozen food section of your market)
1 medium tomato, roughly chopped
1 cup shelled edamame (soy beans)
1/2 cup white wine

4 tablespoons butter
1 tablespoon white miso
1 1/2 tablespoons oyster sauce
1 teaspoon soy sauce
1 teaspoon salt
1 teaspoon pepper
2 tablespoons flour
1 lemon
1/4 cup chopped cilantro

Heat the olive oil in a deep pot over medium-high heat. Add the onion, sausage, and garlic and sauté. You want to render the oil out of the sausage while flavoring the olive oil with the onion and garlic. Cook until the onions are translucent, or about 2–3 minutes.

Add the mussels, tomato, edamame, white wine, 2 tablespoons of the butter, miso, oyster sauce, and soy sauce to the pot and bring to a boil. When the pot reaches a boil, turn down the heat to medium and cover. Cook 4 more minutes or until alcohol is cooked out.

TO FINISH THE DISH

Take the remaining 2 tablespoons of butter and knead the butter with the 2 tablespoons flour until incorporated—this creates a beurre manié, which is used to thicken the sauce and enrich the flavor (see page 176 for tips). Add the beurre manié to the pot and stir constantly until well mixed. Cook 2 minutes more, then remove from heat.

Cut the lemon in half. Squeeze the juice from 1/2 of the lemon over the dish; cut the other 1/2 into wedges, as garnish for individual plates. Divide evenly into 4 large soup bowls. Sprinkle with fresh cilantro and serve.

Black Mussels
with Thai Curry and Pineapple

SERVES 4

Fresh mussels are one of my favorite foods. They require very little cooking time, which means I don't have to wait very long to sit down to a bowl of mussels! In this mussel dish, our deliciously sweet Maui Gold pineapple balances the heat of a curry sauce, introducing a bit of sweetness. This recipe is so simple and easy—you should make it tonight!

White wine can be substituted for sake and lemon zest can be substituted for lemongrass.

—*James McDonald*

1 pound black mussels, anchor beards removed	1 cup diced Maui Gold pineapple
1 tablespoon peanut oil	1 teaspoon minced shallot
1 teaspoon minced ginger	¼ cup sake
2 teaspoons minced garlic	2 cups coconut milk, unsweetened
2 teaspoons red Thai curry paste	1 tablespoon butter
1 tablespoon chopped lemongrass	Salt to taste

In large sauté pan over medium-high heat, add the peanut oil, ginger, garlic, red curry paste, lemongrass, pineapple, and shallots. Sauté for 30 seconds. Add the mussels, sake, coconut milk and butter and cook until the mussels open, which should take about 2 minutes. Remove mussels and place into a serving dish. Season the cooking broth with salt to taste. Pour the sauce over the mussels and dig in!

Bacon-Wrapped 'Ahi with Apple Gastrique

SERVES 4

I usually serve this popular entrée with the Hana Bay Potato Salad on page 57 and the Mountain Apple-Watermelon Radish Slaw on page 56. Both sides highlight the crisp bacon-wrapped 'ahi. Temperatures and textures combine and contrast to create a truly satisfying dish.

—John Cox

---

4 'ahi steaks (approximately 5 ounces each, 2-inches thick), cut from an 'ahi block
4 slices bacon
2 tablespoons coriander seed
2 tablespoons cumin seed
Coarse salt
Freshly ground black pepper
2 cups canola oil

APPLE GASTRIQUE (SWEET AND SOUR GLAZE)
1 cup sugar
¼ cup apple cider vinegar

Hana Bay Potato Salad (see page 57)
Mountain Apple-Watermelon Radish Slaw (see page 56)

TO PREPARE THE 'AHI

Wrap a piece of bacon around the outside of each 'ahi piece. The bacon should be trimmed so it goes around the 'ahi once, with only a slight overlap. Place a tooth-pick where the bacon overlaps to hold it in place.

In a small bowl, combine the coriander and cumin with salt and pepper. Rub the mixture onto both sides of the 'ahi. You can also use Maui Culinary Academy's Thai Basil Sea Salt or your favorite seafood seasoning.

TO PREPARE THE GASTRIQUE

Melt the sugar over high heat in a small saucepan, constantly stirring, for about 1–2 minutes, until golden brown. Remove from heat and add the vinegar. The gas-trique should be a thick syrup. If it is too thick, you can add warm water as necessary. Keep warm until serving.

TO COOK THE 'AHI

Pour the canola oil into a medium-size sauté pan. Heat the oil to 350 degrees and cook the fish for approximately 2 minutes or until the bacon is crisp. Carefully flip the fish and cook for an additional 2 minutes, or until the fish is cooked rare. The fish should still be pink in the center.

TO SERVE

Set out 4 plates and put ½ cup of potato salad in the center of each plate. Slice the 'ahi in half vertically to show the beautiful rare center of the fillet; place it next to the potato salad. Finish the plate by nestling a ¼ cup portion of the slaw against the 'ahi and then drizzling 2 tablespoons of apple gastrique over the dish.

Thai Basil Beef

SERVES 6

Beef from Maui Cattle Company takes center stage in this recipe. If you can't find it in your favorite store, use the freshest, locally raised beef you can find for the best flavor.

Serve pan-fried steaks with a drizzle of oyster sauce and chopped fresh herbs, such as mint, basil, and cilantro, for garnish. This dish is excellent with the Maui Roasted Vegetable Salad on page 63.

Maui Thai Basil Sea Salt—one of the products developed by MCA's Research and Development students—is available for purchase at the Maui Culinary Academy and at gourmet shops throughout the islands.

—*Chris Speere*

---

6 New York or rib-eye steaks, cut into
   6-ounce portions

THAI BASIL MARINADE
2 tablespoons Maui Thai Basil Sea Salt
½ cup soy sauce
½ cup water
¼ cup rice wine

½ cup lime juice
2 stalks lemongrass, smashed
2 thin slices ginger
2 cloves garlic, smashed
1 shallot, sliced thin
2 tablespoons Thai basil, chopped
3 tablespoons cilantro, chopped
¼ cup brown sugar

Put all the marinade ingredients in a bowl and mix thoroughly. Allow the sugar to dissolve completely before you add the beef. Marinate the beef for up to 1 hour.

Heat 2 tablespoons of canola oil in a large heavy sauté pan or iron skillet over high heat until oil just begins to smoke. Carefully put 2 steaks into the hot pan and let them cook over high heat, undisturbed, for 2 minutes on each side. Remove the steaks from the pan and arrange them in the center of a large platter. Repeat the pan-frying process with the remaining 4 steaks. You can also grill the steaks over kiawe (mesquite wood) for a fantastic flavor!

Serve steaks on a large platter family-style. They go great with the Maui Roasted Vegetable Salad on page 63.

Beef Stew with a Pacific-Asian Twist

This dish combines a local, island-style beef stew recipe with basic beans, peanut butter, and raisins. You may be thinking, "This can't work." But it does—and it's delicious!

—*Robert Santos*

2 pounds Maui Cattle Company beef chunks for stew (other beef is fine if you can't find Maui Cattle Company beef at your favorite store)	3 carrots, peeled and cut into large chunks
	2 potatoes, peeled and cut into large chunks
	2 tomatoes, cut into large chunks
	2 teaspoons salt
3 cups water	1 teaspoon black pepper
2 bay leaves	1 can (15-ounce size) pinto or other such beans
2 cloves garlic, chopped	
1 large onion, peeled and cut into large chunks	$\frac{1}{4}$ cup instant potato granules
	$\frac{1}{4}$ cup peanut butter
4 ribs celery, cut into large chunks	$\frac{1}{2}$ cup raisins

Heat a heavy-bottomed pot over medium-high heat until a drop of water, flicked into the pan, "dances" over the bottom. Put a few chunks of beef into the hot pan to brown. Turn the pieces as needed and remove them when they are nicely browned on all sides. This may take about 2 minutes; the beef should be browned to the color of dark toast. Take the browned chunks out of the pan and set them aside in a bowl. Add more beef chunks, brown, and reserve; repeat until you have browned all the beef. Don't try to save time by browning all the pieces at once; the temperature in the pan will drop and the meat will not brown properly.

When all the beef is browned, put it all back into the pot and add the water, bay leaves and garlic. Turn the heat to high heat and bring the beef to a boil; then cover, reduce the heat, and simmer the meat over medium-low heat until beef softens. This may take 45 minutes or longer.

Add the vegetables to the pot. Bring to a boil again and then turn the heat down to medium-low and simmer until just tender, or about 15 more minutes. Add salt and pepper, and cook for approximately 2 more minutes, to develop the flavor.

Add the canned beans, instant potato granules, peanut butter, and raisins. Cook on low heat until the stew is simmering again. Stir well. If the soup is too thin, thicken it with more instant potato granules. Taste and adjust the seasoning, if necessary. Remove the bay leaves before serving. Serve over or with brown rice.

Maui Braised Short Ribs

I love braised foods like short ribs or lamb shanks. They are cooked with time and love. They remind me of Sunday afternoons at grandma's house. When grandma slow-cooked pot roast, the delicious aromas permeated the whole house. I waited impatiently for her to take the roast out of the oven. I wanted to catch that first peek, or better yet, score the crusty end slice that she reserved only for me.

You can use boneless short ribs for this recipe if you prefer. We like the beef from Maui Cattle Company best—it is 100% natural, hormone free, grass fed, and raised locally. But if you can't find it in your favorite store, use the freshest, locally raised beef you can find for the best flavor.

If you are making the short ribs ahead of time, cook the meat and then store it in the braising liquid. When it's time to serve, reheat the liquid-covered meat in the oven or on the stove top. Then proceed to make the sauce as described in the recipe.

For a light and colorful counterpart, serve these melt-in-your-mouth ribs with sauteed diced vegetables, as shown. For heartier fare, pair the ribs with the Velvety Smooth Yukon Gold Potato and Parsnip Purée (see page 81) and some horseradish sour cream or crème fraîche (see page 24).

—*Tom Lelli*

6 pieces short ribs, bone in (7-8 ounces each)	Salt and fresh ground pepper to taste
All-purpose flour, for dredging	3 cups beef or chicken stock
½ cup canola or other neutral oil (you may need a little more)	**MARINADE**
½ cup peeled and chopped carrots (cut into 1-inch pieces)	1 bottle red wine (the Plantation Red from Maui's Tedeschi Winery works well here)
1 cup chopped yellow onion (cut into 1-inch pieces)	1 teaspoon black peppercorns
½ cup chopped celery (cut into 1-inch pieces)	1 bay leaf
	3 sprigs fresh thyme
	4 cloves garlic, roughly chopped

TO PREPARE THE MARINADE

Place the wine, peppercorns, bay leaf and thyme and garlic in a saucepot over medium heat, bring to a simmer, and cook for 5-7 minutes. This burns off the alcohol in the wine. Remove the marinade from the heat and pour through a strainer; take out the garlic and thyme. Cool to room temperature.

When you're sure the mixture has cooled sufficiently—very hot liquid can crack glass—place the meat in a non-reactive glass bowl, pour the marinade over the meat, and refrigerate overnight.

TO PREPARE THE BEEF AND VEGETABLES

Preheat the oven to 325 degrees. Remove the meat from the marinade and reserve the marinade. Pat the meat dry with a paper towel and season all sides with salt and pepper. Dredge the meat in the flour, shaking off the excess.

Pour the oil into a heavy bottom sauté pan; be sure the bottom of the pan is coated. Heat the oil over medium high heat until it begins to smoke slightly. Sear one or two pieces of meat at a time, being careful not to crowd the pan (this causes the pan to cool off, which you don't want to happen). Add more oil as needed while you sear the meat. Cook the meat over high heat for 3 minutes on each side until well-browned, being careful not to burn the flour.

Remove the meat and place it in a heavy casserole or braising pan. Pour off the excess oil from the sauté pan; leave only enough to completely coat the bottom of the pan. Add the carrots, onion, and celery, and sauté for 4–5 minutes over medium high heat or until the vegetables begin to caramelize (become slightly brown).

(recipe continued on page 132)

Remove the vegetables from the sauté pan and add to the meat in the casserole dish. Cover the meat and vegetables with the reserved marinade and the stock. You can add more stock (or water) if needed to just cover the meat. Add the reserved garlic and thyme. Cover the pan tightly with aluminum foil. Cook in the oven for approximately 3 hours, or until the meat begins to fall apart when touched with a fork.

Carefully remove the meat with a large slotted spoon. Put it on a serving platter and keep warm.

TO FINISH THE DISH

Skim the fat from the braising liquid and strain it into a saucepan. Discard the vegetables. Over medium heat, simmer until the liquid is reduced by ½ or ¾. Season the sauce with salt and pepper and serve with the ribs.

❀ MEAT · PORK ❀

Maui Gold Pineapple Glazed Baby Back Ribs

SERVES 6

If you like your meat moist and tender, this recipe is the best. This dish features two uniquely Maui products: our luscious Maui Gold pineapple, developed and grown by Maui Pineapple Company, and our world-renowned Maui Brand Natural White Cane Sugar. The pineapple marinade adds sweetness and a rich caramel color to the ribs.

Select ribs that are trimmed of excess fat (or trim them yourself) and avoid turning the ribs too often once they are on the grill.

—*Chris Speere*

4 racks of baby back ribs (approximately 3½ to 4 pounds total)

MARINADE
1 cup diced Maui Gold pineapple
3 tablespoons Maui Brand Natural White Cane Sugar
1 tablespoon curry powder
1 teaspoon Chinese five-spice powder

½ teaspoon cayenne pepper
½ teaspoon salt
¼ teaspoon black pepper
¼ cup soy sauce
2 tablespoons lime juice
2 tablespoons rum
¼ cup ketchup
1 tablespoon minced garlic

Purée the pineapple in a blender or a food processor. In a large bowl, combine the puréed pineapple with the rest of the marinade ingredients and mix well. Add the ribs and turn them until they are well-coated with the marinade. Cover and marinate for up to 12 hours in the refrigerator.

Remove the ribs from the refrigerator 30 minutes before roasting them. Preheat oven to 375 degrees.

Remove the ribs from the marinade and brush off any pieces of garlic and ginger that have clung to the ribs. Save the marinade. Wrap each rack of ribs tightly in foil and place the foil packages in a baking pan. Roast the ribs for 1½ hours.

In a small saucepan, bring the marinade to a boil and simmer for 3–5 minutes or until it becomes slightly syrupy. Keep warm.

Remove the baked ribs from the foil and place them on a hot barbecue or indoor gas grill. Grill the ribs at low heat, brushing them with the marinade every 2 minutes. Cook on one side for 10 minutes. Turn the ribs over and resume brushing with marinade every 2 minutes for another 10 minutes. The ribs should be brown and glazed.

TO SERVE

Cut the ribs apart through the joints, and serve hot…with plenty of napkins.

Pork Tenderloin
with Granny Smith Apple Compote

SERVES 6

When I explain to my students why certain dishes work so well, the flavor combination of salty and sweet is one of the examples I use. Pork and apples are an ever-popular salty-sweet treat. In this dish, we use the bacon as the salty counterpoint to the sweet apple compote. The pork tenderloin rubbed with garlic and rosemary adds complexity and delicious flavor.

Pork tenderloins are available in most supermarkets and are easy to trim. You can use any tart apples for the apple compote.

Try serving this dish with Velvety Smooth Yukon Gold Potato and Parsnip Purée (see page 81) and your favorite vegetables.

—*Tom Lelli*

1½ pounds pork tenderloins
6 pieces bacon or pancetta, thinly sliced
2 tablespoons extra virgin olive oil
2 cloves garlic, minced
1 sprig fresh rosemary, chopped
Salt and fresh ground pepper to taste
¼ cup canola oil
6 toothpicks

APPLE COMPOTE
5 Granny Smith apples, peeled, cored, and cut into large dice
1 cup + 1 tablespoon brown sugar
1 cinnamon stick
½ vanilla bean, split and scraped
1 dried chipotle or Ancho chilli (optional)
4 tablespoons butter
2 cups water
Salt to taste

TO MARINATE THE PORK

Trim the silver skin off the pork tenderloins. (The silver skin is a tough white membrane found on the outside of the tenderloin.) Cut the tenderloins into six equal portions. Lay the tenderloins flat on a cutting board and cut into medallions, small round steaks like filet mignons. Wrap a piece of bacon around the outside of each pork medallion. The bacon should be trimmed so it goes around the pork once, with only a slight overlap. Place a toothpick where the bacon overlaps to hold it in place.

In a small bowl, mix the olive oil, garlic and rosemary and then rub the mixture onto the pork medallions. Refrigerate covered for 1 hour.

TO PREPARE THE APPLE COMPOTE

Preheat the oven to 350 degrees. Place the apple pieces, sugar, cinnamon sticks, vanilla skins, butter, water, salt, and optional chilli in an oven proof casserole dish

(recipe continued on page 136)

and cover with a lid. Bake in the oven for 15-20 minutes or until the apples are tender, but not too soft.

Remove the cinnamon stick, chilli, and vanilla bean skins from the apples. Keep warm.

TO SEAR THE PORK
Preheat an ovenproof sauté pan or skillet over medium heat. Season the pork with salt and pepper. Place the canola oil in the pan and add the pork when the oil is hot, being careful not to crowd the pan. Sear the pork until brown, about 3 minutes per side, then turn the portions on their sides so the bacon cooks, too.

You can finish cooking the pork over medium heat or place it in the oven for 10–15 minutes depending on how well done you like your pork.

TO SERVE
When the pork is finished, remove the toothpicks and serve the pork with the warm apple compote. To round out the presentation, serve with grilled zucchini, asparagus and carrots.

Miso-Sake Braised Pork Belly on Edamame and Shiitake Mushroom Ragoût

SERVES 4

The first time I ever tried braised pork belly was at Masa's restaurant in San Francisco. It was served as an *amuse bouche* (a bite-sized appetizer served before the meal), and it literally melted in my mouth. As a result of that experience, I developed and served this dish as the *amuse bouche* course for a 2005 dinner celebrating Maui Culinary Academy's gold medal in a national competition.

—*Kyle Kawakami*

1 piece pork belly (approximately 1 pound)
1 tablespoon peanut oil
½ cup finely sliced green onion, cut on the bias

BRAISING LIQUID
2 cups water
⅓ cup sugar
⅓ cup soy sauce
⅓ cup white miso
1 cup sake
2 cloves garlic, smashed

1 tablespoon sliced fresh ginger
1 star anise pod
1 teaspoon whole black peppercorns

EDAMAME AND SHIITAKE MUSHROOM RAGOÛT
1 tablespoon butter
1 teaspoon minced garlic
1 teaspoon minced ginger
2 cups sliced fresh shiitake mushrooms
1 cup peeled edamame (soy beans)
½ cup julienned leeks (whites only)
2 cups sliced baby bok choy

Cut pork belly lengthwise into four 5 x 3 x 1¼-inch-thick pieces. Heat the peanut oil in a heavy sauté pan over high heat. Add the pork belly portions to the sauté pan skin side down and cook for 3–4 minutes per side until they are golden brown. Remove the pork from the sauté pan, place it on a platter, and hold at room temperature.

In a large heavy saucepot with a tight fitting lid, combine all of the braising ingredients and bring to a boil over medium heat. Add the browned pork belly to the braising liquid, making sure that the pieces are completely covered with the braising liquid. Return the liquid to a boil, then reduce the heat to low and simmer covered for 2 hours, skimming off any foam that develops during the simmering process. Once the pork belly pieces are tender, remove them from the braising liquid and slice each portion of pork belly into 3 equal square slices. Keep the pork hot until ready to serve.

TO PREPARE THE RAGOÛT

Heat a medium-size sauté pan over medium heat. Melt the butter and sauté the garlic and ginger for one minute. Add the shiitake mushrooms, edamame, and leeks, and sauté for 2–3 minutes. Add the baby bok choy and sauté until it is wilted or approximately one more minute. Add ½ cup of the braising liquid to the ragoût and mix to combine.

TO SERVE

This dish is best served in attractive individual bowls, which allow each person to enjoy the intense aroma of the braising liquid. Spoon ¼ cup of the ragoût into the center of each bowl. Place 3 slices of pork belly on the ragoût and drizzle ¼ of the remaining braising liquid over the pork. Top each bowl with a sprinkling of sliced green onion.

Grilled Lemon Chicken with Fusilli

SERVES 6

This light pasta dish is quick and easy; you can cook most of it on the barbecue. You can also use a grill pan on your stovetop. Have all the ingredients ready and at room temperature so that you can toss the pasta together at the last minute. Serve it family style with a salad and some crusty bread.

We make this with fusilli but you can substitute your own favorite dried pasta. I recommend that you choose something that "holds" onto the sauce; that's why fusilli works so well. Experiment with adding garden vegetables like eggplant and asparagus. You can also omit the chicken for a delicious vegetarian dish.

—*Tom Lelli*

GRILLED LEMON CHICKEN
6 boneless chicken breasts
   (approximately 6 ounces each),
   skin-on
3 sprigs of chopped rosemary
1 recipe lemon vinaigrette (see page 9)
Salt and black pepper

PASTA
1 pound of your favorite dried pasta
1 zucchini, cut into ¼-inch thick
   slices for grilling
1 yellow squash, cut into ¼-inch
   slices for grilling

1 red onion, cut into ½ inch slices
1 tablespoon olive oil
1 cup chopped sun-dried tomatoes in
   olive oil, at room temperature
2 tablespoons extra virgin olive oil
6 cloves of garlic, minced
1 cup white wine
1 cup chicken stock
1 cup roughly chopped fresh basil
6 ounces of goat cheese, at room
   temperature (we like the selection
   from Maui's Surfing Goat Dairy)

Marinate the chicken for at least 2 hours in the vinaigrette and rosemary.

Cook the pasta until it is al dente (or to your preferred firmness). Set the pasta aside, covered, at room temperature. If you won't be using the pasta immediately, you might want to toss it with a teaspoon of olive oil so that it does not stick together.

Preheat the barbecue. Rub the zucchini, squash and red onion with the 1 tablespoon of olive oil and season with salt and pepper. Be careful not to use too much oil; this could cause the fire to flare up and "blacken" the vegetables. Grill the onions for 3 minutes a side; the rest of the vegetables will only need 2 minutes on each side. Set the vegetables aside and let them cool. Then chop the vegetables into bite-size pieces.

Remove the chicken breasts from the marinade; shake the excess marinade back into the bowl. Season with salt and pepper. Grill the chicken on the barbecue until it is just done, or for approximately 4 minutes on each side.

Heat the 2 tablespoons of extra virgin olive oil in a large sauté pan over low heat. Add the chopped garlic and "sweat" it for 1 minute. Be careful not to let the garlic get brown. If it does get brown, it will be bitter.

Turn the heat up to medium high, deglaze the pan with the white wine and chicken stock, then cook until the liquid is reduced by half. This will take 3–5 minutes. Add all the chopped vegetables and toss them in the pan until they are warm, or for about 1 minute. Add the pasta, basil, and goat cheese and toss for another 1–2 minutes. Season with salt and pepper and serve with the warm chicken.

For additional color, you can make a red sauce by combining a few oven-dried tomatoes (see page 2) with a little warm chicken stock and fresh herbs in a food processor. Use as an optional garnish on the plate.

Hulihuli Style Roasted Chicken

If you live in Hawai'i, you're probably familiar with traditional hulihuli roasted chicken. Hulihuli means "to turn" in Hawaiian; this chicken is smoked on a constantly turning rotisserie over a charcoal fire. You can see it being prepared on weekends—often in parking lots!—for big family gatherings and local-style fundraisers. Hulihuli chicken is sweet, smoky, and utterly delicious. It's difficult to duplicate in a home kitchen without a rotisserie and some kiawe (mesquite) charcoal. This recipe, however, gets pretty close to the original and is a picnic favorite with our family.

Serve it with macaroni salad, tossed green salad, French fries, coleslaw, and grilled fresh corn. Oh, and if you're local, like my family, you know you gotta have your white rice too!

—Darryl Dela Cruz

---

2 broiler chickens (about 2 pounds each), cut in half, backbones removed

MARINADE
2 cups soy sauce
2 cups water
1$\frac{3}{4}$ cups sugar
2 tablespoons sliced and crushed ginger
1 tablespoon liquid smoke
$\frac{1}{2}$ cup sliced green onion

Combine all the marinade ingredients. Mix until the sugar is completely dissolved. Add the halved chickens and marinate (covered) overnight in the refrigerator.

Heat a grill pan over medium heat. Place the chickens in the pan, skin side down. Cook until nicely browned, about 8–10 minutes. Turn and cook for another 8–10 minutes. Check for doneness by piercing the inner thigh with a fork; if the juices run clear rather than bloody, the chicken is done.

Mochiko Chicken

This local-style fried chicken is made with mochiko or rice flour, a staple food for many island families. You've probably eaten rice flour in bibinka or butter mochi; now you can try it with chicken. If you have a home table-top fryer, this chicken is even easier to make. Enjoy it often!

Serve with rice and macaroni salad for a broke-da-mouth lunch. You'll probably overeat so be sure you have time for a nap afterwards! This dish is also a great party pūpū. Cut the chicken into small, nugget-size pieces before you fry them; they'll disappear faster than uncle's smoke meat. Just the thing when every one is sitting around talking story.

For more tips on deep frying, see page 177.

—Nalu Castillo

---

2 cups mochiko flour
2 cups sugar
1 cup soy sauce
3 large eggs
¾ cup thinly sliced green onion

3 cloves minced garlic
2–3 pounds of boneless chicken, cut
  into ¾ x 1½-inch pieces
3 cups oil

Mix the flour and sugar in a large bowl. Add the soy sauce and eggs; mix thoroughly. Add the garlic and green onions and mix again. Put the chicken pieces in the bowl and, with cooking chopsticks, tongs, even your hands if you wish, coat the chicken pieces completely with the mixture. Let the chicken marinate in the refrigerator for at least 2 hours. If you'd like, you can leave the marinating chicken in the refrigerator, covered, for up to 3 days.

Heat the oil to 325 degrees and fry the chicken in batches until it is golden brown, or about 7–10 minutes. Drain on paper towels and serve.

Roasted Chicken with Maui Arugula & Macadamia Nut Pesto

Our family's Haʻikū garden produces an abundance of arugula several times a year. We make a flavorful pesto from the arugula and enjoy its spicy and robust flavor all year 'round. To give the dish a dash of extra flavor, let the chicken rest for 20 minutes after you take it from the oven, then rub it with more pesto before carving.

This recipe also works well with turkey; either preparation is perfect for dinner parties.

—*Chris Speere*

---

2 chickens (3–4 pounds each) **Salt and pepper**	**Maui Arugula & Macadamia Nut Pesto** **(see page 14)**

Season the chickens inside and out with salt and pepper. Rub the chickens with pesto inside and out. Save some pesto for finishing the dish. Let the chickens sit in the refrigerator—in a covered bowl or pan—for 1 hour.

Preheat the oven to 375 degrees. Remove the chickens from the refrigerator and place in a roasting pan. Roast the chickens at 375 degrees, basting every 15 minutes. The cooking time will vary from approximately 1 to 1½ hours. You can use a meat thermometer to test for doneness. Insert the thermometer into a chicken thigh; if it registers 180 degrees, the meat is done. Alternatively, you can puncture the thigh meat with a sharp paring knife; if the juices run clear rather than bloody, the chicken is cooked.

Allow the chickens to rest at room temperature for at least 10 minutes before carving.

Chicken Adobo Stew

I enjoy recipes that are simple to make, flavorful and easy to serve. This is the ultimate local-style comfort food and perfect for family potlucks!

You can also make this dish with pork. Cut pork shoulder into 1-inch cubes and substitute for the chicken. Follow the same recipe directions but simmer the stew under low heat for two hours.

Fresh watercress salad with tofu and tomatoes is a perfect complement to this dish.

—Karen Tanaka

---

3 pounds chicken thighs, boneless, skinless, and cut into large chunks
$1/3$ to $1/2$ cup cider vinegar
$1/2$ cup soy sauce
6 cloves garlic, minced
3 to 4 bay leaves
2 teaspoons black peppercorns
$1/4$ cup olive oil
6 carrots, cut into large dice

4 medium new potatoes, cut into large dice
1 large onion, chopped fine
1 cup fresh green beans, cut into 1- or 2-inch pieces
6 stalks celery, cut into 1- or 2-inch pieces
1 to 2 cans chicken broth

Marinate the chicken pieces in the vinegar, soy sauce, garlic, bay leaves, and peppercorns for at least 1 hour, in the refrigerator.

Lightly coat the bottom of a large pot with olive oil. Remove the bay leaves and peppercorns from the marinade. Add the chicken (including the marinade) to the pot together with the carrots, potatoes and onion. Cook over high heat for 5 minutes or until the chicken pieces are lightly browned. Add a little chicken broth if it is needed to prevent sticking. Add the green beans, celery, and chicken broth. If you have used some broth from the first can to prevent sticking, add the rest of the can. If you like a thinner stew, you can add the second can of broth as well. Cook the stew over medium high heat for an additional 10–15 minutes until the chicken is thoroughly cooked and the vegetables are fork-tender.

Serve hot from the pot with steamed rice.

Poêle of Chicken with Preserved Lemon, Garlic, and Rosemary

SERVES 4

There is nothing as simple and satisfying as a roasted chicken, especially when it is served with root vegetables that have soaked up the cooking juices from the pan. We give this dish a twist with a seasoning of Moroccan preserved lemon, garlic, and rosemary. We do not serve this roasted chicken in our Leis Family Class Act Restaurant, but it is one of our favorite staff meals. It shows our students how simple a great dish can be.

Make sure the potatoes are small enough so they finish cooking at the same time as the vegetables. Small waxy potatoes are best; try Yukon Gold, Red B, or Fingerling potatoes. If washed well, these can be cooked without peeling. Peeled russet potatoes will work, if cut into smaller pieces. You can also use (or add) root vegetables such as turnips. Regular onions can be replaced with pearl onions. You can use lemon zest in place of the preserved lemon, if you prefer.

Serve with a light tossed salad.

—Tom Lelli

---

2 whole chickens, 2½ to 3 pounds each
Juice of 2 lemons
4 tablespoons extra virgin olive oil
1 preserved lemon, pulp removed, rinsed (see the Preserved Lemons recipe on page 3)
8 cloves garlic, whole
3 sprigs fresh thyme, chopped
1 sprig fresh rosemary leaves, chopped, plus 1 whole sprig
1 onion, yellow or white, cut in 1-inch pieces

1 lemon cut in half
1 carrot, peeled, cut into 1-inch pieces
2 parsnips, peeled, cut in 1-inch pieces
1 celery root, peeled, cut in 1-inch pieces
6 small whole waxy potatoes such as Yukon gold or Red B
12 tablespoons butter, melted (1½ sticks)
Salt and fresh ground pepper, to taste

TO PREPARE THE MARINADE AND CHICKEN

Put the lemon juice, olive oil, preserved lemon, and garlic in a blender or food processor. Add a few drops of water to facilitate blending if necessary. Blend for about 30 seconds. All ingredients should be finely chopped and well combined. Put the mixture in a bowl and stir in chopped thyme and chopped rosemary.

Rub the lemon garlic mixture over each chicken, outside and inside. Carefully pull up the skin on the chicken breasts and rub some marinade on the breast meat under the skin. Place a half lemon, a piece of onion, and half rosemary sprig in the cavity of each chicken.

Truss the chicken with butcher's twine. Tuck the wing tips under the front of the chicken. Take a piece of butcher's twine 3 times the length of a chicken and place the middle of the string under the tail. Bring the ends up and around the end of each leg crossing the twine as you pull down. Continue pulling the ends of the twine around the chicken and over the wings so the legs and wings are pulled in close to the body and tie in the front at the base of the neck. This will ensure the chicken holds its shape during cooking.

Refrigerate covered for 3 hours or overnight.

TO ROAST THE CHICKEN

Preheat the oven to 350 degrees. Place the vegetables in a roasting pan that is large enough to hold both chickens without touching each other and also to leave an inch or two between the chickens and the sides of the pan. Toss the vegetables with melted butter and season lightly with salt and pepper. Season the chicken with salt and black pepper; go light on the salt, as the preserved lemon added salt to the marinade. Place the chickens on the bed of vegetables, cover the pan with a lid or with foil, and roast the chickens until they are done. This should take approximately 1½ to 2 hours depending on the size of the chickens.

To test for doneness, you can check with a food thermometer. Insert the thermometer in the chicken thigh; the thigh should be 165 degrees. You can also use a paring knife. Stick the knife into the thigh; if the thigh seeps clear liquid, it's done.

Baste the chickens with fat from the pan every 20 minutes. Remove the lid or the foil for the last 30 minutes of cooking to allow the chickens to brown. You can add a little water or chicken stock to the bottom of the pan if all the juices from the chicken evaporate during the last 30 minutes. This will prevent the vegetables from burning.

TO SERVE

Remove the chickens from the pan, cut them into quarters and serve with the vegetables and drippings from the roasting pan.

Duck Confit with Lentils and Caramelized Pearl Onions

SERVES 4

Duck confit is a classic culinary preparation. The duck meat is cured in salt, then cooked very slowly in its own fat. The meat comes out so flavorful, it is worth the time and effort to create this special dish.

—*Claude Gaty*

6 duck legs, which can be bought
    separately from whole ducks
2 tablespoons kosher salt
$\frac{1}{2}$ teaspoon black peppercorns
1 teaspoon cracked juniper berries
1 bay leaf, crumbled
1 tablespoon olive oil
3 cups rendered duck fat, which can
    be purchased in 8-ounce containers
1 tablespoon chopped fresh thyme
2 cloves garlic, sliced
1 sprig rosemary
1 sprig parsley

BOUQUET GARNI
1 large outer stalk celery
4 stalks parsley, whole stems with
    leaves
1 sprig thyme
1 bay leaf
3 leeks

LENTILS
2 cups French lentils
1 quart water
1 teaspoon salt
$\frac{1}{2}$ teaspoon pepper
1 sprig thyme
1 bay leaf
1 clove garlic, minced
$\frac{1}{2}$ cup finely diced carrots
$\frac{1}{2}$ cup finely diced onions
$\frac{1}{2}$ cup finely diced celery

CARAMELIZED PEARL ONIONS
16 white pearl onions
2 cups water
3 tablespoons unsalted butter
$\frac{1}{2}$ teaspoon salt
1 teaspoon sugar

TO PREPARE THE DUCK

Tie all the Bouquet Garni ingredients together with kitchen twine. Arrange the duck legs on a sheet pan lined with parchment paper and season both sides with salt, pepper, juniper berries and crumbled bay leaf. Cover the pan with tin foil and marinate the duck legs overnight in the refrigerator.

In a large heavy skillet over moderate heat, sear the duck legs in the olive oil, starting with the skin side down, until the meat is golden brown. This should take approximately 4 minutes on each side. Add the duck fat, Bouquet Garni, thyme, garlic, rosemary, and parsley to the skillet and slowly bring the confit to a boil. Turn off the heat, cover the skillet, and place the dish in a 200 degree oven. Cook for 4 hours. Remove the skillet from the oven and transfer the contents—including all the duck fat—into a large heatproof container to cool. Set aside until the final assembly of the dish.

TO PREPARE THE LENTILS

Rinse the lentils 3 times under cold water. Place the lentils, the quart of water and all the remaining ingredients into a large saucepot. Bring the lentils to a boil over moderate heat. Skim the foam from surface and simmer lentils until they are tender, or for approximately 40 minutes. Keep the lentils warm until the final assembly of the dish.

TO PREPARE THE ONIONS

Place all the ingredients into a large saucepot. Cook the pearl onions over low heat for approximately 10 minutes or until all the liquid has evaporated and the onions look lightly caramelized.

TO ASSEMBLE THE DISH

Remove the duck legs from the fat, place them skin side up onto a baking sheet, and roast in a 425 degree oven for approximately 12–25 minutes, or until the skin is crisp.

TO SERVE

Spoon ½ cup of lentils onto each plate. Place a crispy duck leg on top of the lentils and garnish each plate with 4 caramelized pearl onions.

DESSERTS

The first thing you see when you arrive to Maui is the famous Pu'unene sugar mill. The centerpiece for sugar production on Maui for generations, the mill not only preserves the rich history of the island's sugar plantation life, it also continues to produce our famous sugar. Pastry chefs appreciate good quality sugar for making their baked treats and spectacular sweets, so don't skimp on the good stuff when you're making these recipes. From homegrown pies and breads to sumptuous crème brûlée and cakes, these desserts are an excellent way to satisfy your sweet tooth and end a delicious *Taste of Maui* meal.

Healthy Sweet Potato Haupia Pie

MAKES ONE PIE, WHICH USUALLY SERVES 8

I invented this recipe for several close friends who are diabetic and love coconut and sweet potato. Now they can enjoy a dessert that doesn't make them feel guilty!

—*Elaine Rothermel*

SWEET POTATO FILLING

2 pounds sweet potatoes, peeled and cut into quarters
1 cup skim milk
1 teaspoon vanilla extract
2 tablespoons I Can't Believe It's Not Butter™, softened (ICBINB for short)
1 teaspoon sugar substitute
1 low fat graham cracker piecrust (available at all supermarkets)

HAUPIA TOPPING

3 cups fat-free evaporated milk or regular fat free milk
Water, if needed
½ cup cornstarch
1 teaspoon coconut extract
8 teaspoons sugar substitute

TO PREPARE THE FILLING

Steam or boil the sweet potatoes until soft, which should take 30–40 minutes. Drain the potatoes and put them in a mixing bowl. When the potatoes have cooled to room temperature, add the milk, vanilla extract, ICBINB, and the sugar substitute and mix well. The mixture should be the consistency of mashed potatoes. Spoon the mixture into the piecrust.

TO PREPARE THE HAUPIA TOPPING

Combine the milk and the cornstarch in a saucepan. The mixture should be very smooth; if it is lumpy, try adding some water and stirring again. Cook over medium heat, stirring constantly, until the mixture starts to thicken. Lower the heat and continue to cook and stir for another 5 minutes. Turn off the heat and stir in the coconut extract and sugar substitute. Cool for 15 minutes.

TO SERVE

Spread haupia topping over the sweet potato filling and serve.

Lemon Macadamia Nut Biscotti

Citrus and macadamia nuts give this biscotti a local twist. These cookies go perfectly with the Lemongrass Crème Brûlée on page 170.

—*Teresa Shurilla*

16 tablespoons (2 sticks) unsalted butter	3 ½ cups bread flour or all-purpose flour
1 cup + ½ cup Maui Brand Natural White Cane Sugar	2 teaspoons baking powder
2 large eggs	¼ teaspoon nutmeg
1½ teaspoons vanilla extract	½ teaspoon salt
¼ teaspoon lemon extract	1 can of macadamia nuts (4-ounce size), wholes and halves

Cream together the butter and 1 cup of the sugar. This can be done with a spoon or a hand mixer but it's easiest, of course, with a stand mixer. Slowly add the eggs, vanilla, and lemon extract.

In a separate bowl, sift together the dry ingredients. Stir the dry mixture into the butter mixture using a plastic spatula.

Stir the macadamia nut halves into the dough and mold it into a rectangle that measures 6 x 3 inches. Freeze the dough on a cookie sheet lined with parchment baking paper. When the dough is completely set, which should take approximately 2 hours, sprinkle the top with the remaining ½ cup sugar and bake the biscotti dough at 350 degrees for approximately 30–35 minutes, or until golden brown. Remove the slab from the oven and let it cool for at least 1 hour.

With a serrated bread knife, cut the slab of baked biscotti dough into slices ¼-inch to ½-inch thick. Put the slices back on the cookie sheet and bake them in a preheated 350-degree oven for an additional 10 minutes. The biscotti should be delightfully crisp and crunchy. Store it in an air-tight container.

Mango Bread

This is one of my favorite homestyle recipes. I learned to make it from friends and relatives, and have revised it over the years until it's as good as it can possibly be. I used this (and other homestyle recipes) when we prepared the Federally Funded JTPA (Job Training Employment Act) lunches. We made those lunches in our old kitchen for more than twenty summers. The good ol' days!

Island mangoes can vary widely in quality. Some of our best mango bread was made from the delicious mangoes Chef Bobby Santos would bring from his home in Olowalu.

Serve warm with freshly whipped cream and sprinkled with nutmeg and cinnamon.

—Karen Tanaka

2 cups all-purpose flour	2 cups finely chopped fresh mango
2 teaspoons baking soda	¾ cup neutral oil like canola oil
½ teaspoon salt	3 eggs, beaten
2 teaspoons cinnamon	1 teaspoon vanilla
2 cups Maui Brand Natural White Sugar	½ cup raisins
	½ cup chopped walnuts (optional)

Preheat oven to 325 degrees. Line 2 loaf pans with waxed paper. Some cooks grease the pan first, add the paper, and grease again. Other cooks just line the pans with paper. Follow your favorite method here.

Sift together the flour, baking soda, salt, cinnamon, and sugar into a large bowl. Make a well in the center of the dry ingredients and add the mango, oil, beaten eggs, and vanilla. Mix well, then fold in the raisins and walnuts. Split the batter evenly between the 2 loaf pans and let the pans stand at room temperature for 20 minutes. Then place the pans into the preheated oven and bake for approximately 1 hour, or until the top of the mango bread is golden brown and firm to the touch.

Mango Clafouti

A clafouti is a sweet baked pancake made with seasonal fruit. Sadly enough, many people have never heard of this French dessert. I believe the dish is too good to be missed. It's full of fresh fruit flavor and is very versatile.

You can also use any fresh berries or stone fruits (such as peaches, plums, or nectarines) in this recipe. They all taste incredibly good. Serve clafouti with a high-quality ice cream—Maui's own Roselani Tropics Mango 'n Cream works wonderfully here—or freshly whipped cream.

—Jeremy Choo

---

1 cup fresh mango, diced
1½ cups milk
¼ cup + ¼ cup Maui Brand Natural
  White Sugar
Pinch of salt
1 teaspoon vanilla extract

2 tablespoons Maui Dark Rum
2 eggs
¼ cup all-purpose flour
Powdered sugar, as needed
Butter, to grease ramekins

Preheat oven to 350 degrees. Coat 4 ramekins (4-ounce size) or individual muffin tins with a thin layer of butter. Divide the mangoes into 4 equal portions. Place each portion into one ramekin and set the ramekins aside.

In a large saucepot, combine the milk, ¼ cup sugar, salt, vanilla extract, and rum. Bring to a simmer over moderate heat until the sugar is dissolved, which should take approximately 3 minutes.

In a small bowl whisk together the eggs, flour and the remaining ¼ cup sugar until the mixture is thick and creamy; again, this should take approximately 3 minutes.

Temper the two mixtures together by gradually adding about half of the hot milk mixture into the egg mixture, whisking constantly. Add the remaining hot milk mixture to the egg mixture, and whisk to combine. Then pour the entire mixture over the mangoes, making sure to divide the mixture equally among the 4 ramekins.

Place the filled ramekins into a 9 x 13-inch ovenproof pan or container. Fill with hot water until the water level is ¾ of the way up the ramekins. This creates a water bath, or bain marie (see tip on page 179). Carefully place the bain marie into the oven.

Bake for 15–17 minutes, or until the clafoutis are set and the tops are light golden brown. Remove the pan from the oven and the ramekins from the hot water bath.

TO SERVE

Dust the tops of the clafouti with powdered sugar and serve warm. Garnish with a scoop of Roselani Mango 'n Cream ice cream or a dollop of whipped cream.

Apple Cake

Some of my earliest childhood memories are of rainy days spent baking with my mother. She was a terrific baker and I'm sure my utter delight in the discipline comes directly from her. I was a young adult before I knew there was such a thing as a packaged cake mix—nothing of the kind ever made an appearance in our house. My mother's handwritten recipes are some of my greatest treasures.

She exchanged many recipes with my grandmother and my aunties, also good cooks. This apple cake is one dessert they all used to make. One of my cousins recently confided to me that he had always liked my mother's apple cake best. Me too.

—*Bonnie Friedman*

4 tablespoons (½ stick) unsalted butter	½ teaspoon salt
1 cup light brown sugar, packed	3 teaspoons baking powder
2 large apples (Granny Smith or other tart, firm apples work best), peeled, cored and sliced	⅓ cup shortening
	⅓ cup sugar
	2 eggs, well beaten
½ cup raisins	½ teaspoon vanilla
1½ cups all-purpose flour, sifted	⅔ cup water

Preheat oven to 350 degrees. Melt the butter in the baking pan. Add the brown sugar and stir until the sugar is completely dissolved. Set aside to cool.

Place the apple slices on top of the butter mixture and sprinkle with raisins. Sift the flour, salt and baking powder together. Cream the shortening with the sugar until light and fluffy. Add the eggs and the vanilla. Add the sifted dry ingredients and water alternately and mix until combined. Pour the mixture over the apples.

Bake for 40–50 minutes, until golden brown. Turn out onto a serving plate immediately. Serve warm, or at room temperature, with Roselani Tropics Hawaiian Vanilla Bean ice cream.

Raspberry White Chocolate Scones

When our beautiful new Pā'ina Culinary Arts Building first opened in 2003, I started making these scones for our food court. They are now so popular I dare not run out!

—*Teresa Shurilla*

5 cups all-purpose flour
¾ cup + 2 tablespoons Maui Brand
    Natural White Cane Sugar
1 tablespoon baking powder
1 teaspoon baking soda
½ teaspoon salt
16 tablespoons (2 sticks) unsalted
    butter, chilled, cut into small pieces
2 eggs

¾ cup buttermilk
1 cup white chocolate chips
⅓ cup raspberry jam

EGG WASH
1 egg yolk
2 tablespoons buttermilk

TO PREPARE THE DOUGH

Put the flour, ¾ cup sugar, baking soda, baking powder, and salt into a mixing bowl. Toss or stir these ingredients until they are well blended. Using two knives, a pastry cutter, or even your fingers, cut the butter into the flour until the mixture resembles cornmeal. Whisk the eggs and the buttermilk together and pour the egg mixture into the flour and butter mix. Mix lightly until the liquid and dry ingredients are thoroughly mixed and form a ball of dough. Wrap the dough ball in plastic and refrigerate it for a minimum of 1 hour.

TO ASSEMBLE THE SCONES

After the dough has chilled, roll it out into a 10-inch diameter circle with a rolling pin. Spread the jam over the top of the circle of dough, then sprinkle the chocolate chips evenly over the surface. Working around the perimeter (outside edge) of the circle, fold the outside of the dough over the top of the chocolate chips and the jam. Pinch the edges together so that they gather up into the center of the circle. You should end up with another circle, but one that is smaller and thicker. Flip the dough over and cut it into 8 equal triangles. Mix the egg wash and brush it onto the tops of the triangles. Sprinkle the tops generously with the remaining 2 tablespoons of sugar. (White sugar will do, if that's all you have, but I prefer to use Maui Brand Natural White Cane Sugar, which has larger crystals).

Bake at 350 degrees for 25–30 minutes or until light golden brown.

Grandma Bogue's Apple Pie

MAKES ONE 9-INCH PIE, WHICH SERVES 6 TO 8
(ACCORDING TO MY BROTHER-IN-LAW, IT SERVES ONE!)

When I was a young girl, I watched my Grandma Hazel whip up wonderful pies, cakes and custards. She was the inspiration for my career. I still make this pie exactly the way she showed me.

—*Teresa Shurilla*

FLAKY PIE DOUGH

4 cups all-purpose flour

$1\frac{1}{4}$ teaspoons salt

11 tablespoons (1 stick plus 3 tablespoons) unsalted butter, chilled, cut into small pieces

6 tablespoons shortening, chilled, cut into small pieces

7 tablespoons ice water (with the ice cubes removed)

APPLE PIE FILLING

5–6 medium Granny Smith apples ($3\frac{3}{4}$ cups when sliced)

$1\frac{3}{4}$ cups sugar

$\frac{1}{3}$ cup all-purpose flour

$1\frac{1}{2}$ teaspoons cinnamon

$\frac{3}{4}$ teaspoon ground ginger

$\frac{1}{4}$ teaspoon ground cloves

3 tablespoons butter, cut into "pats"

TO PREPARE THE PASTRY

Put the flour, salt, cold butter and shortening in a mixing bowl. Gently cut the fat into the flour with a pastry cutter. You can also mix the fat and flour by rubbing it together between your fingers. Mix until the fat pieces are the size of baby lima beans. Leaving the fat in larger pieces results in a flakier crust. Pour the cold water into the bowl and mix the ingredients until they form a dough that sticks together. Do not overwork the dough or it will be tough. If there is time, refrigerate the dough for about 15–20 minutes; it is easier to roll the dough when it is cold. If there isn't time for this step, you can roll it out immediately.

Cut the dough in half. Place it on a smooth surface—your clean counter, a pastry mat, a marble or granite pastry slab if you have one—dusted with flour. With a rolling pin, flatten each half into a circle (a disc) of even thickness. You'll need a circle approximately 10-inches in diameter for the bottom crust and an 11–12-inch circle for the top. You may need to sprinkle some flour on the top of the dough to keep it from sticking to the rolling pin. Lift the dough for the bottom crust into the pie pan; be sure that it's centered in the pan. You can lift the crust without tearing it if you roll the crust around the rolling pin, then unroll the dough into the pan.

(recipe continued on page 156)

Preheat oven to 350 degrees. Peel, core and slice the apples. Toss the sliced apples in a mixing bowl with the sugar, flour, cinnamon, ginger, and cloves. Put the filling in the unbaked pie shell and dot the top of the filling with the pats of butter. Cover the pie with the larger upper crust and crimp the edges of the two crusts together. Cut slashes or steam vents in the top. I like to brush the top crust with a little water and sprinkle Maui Brand Natural White Cane Sugar on top; this gives the crust some extra texture.

TO BAKE THE PIE

Bake for approximately 1 hour and 15 minutes, or until the filling begins to bubble from the top of the pie where the steam vents were cut.

TO SERVE

I love to serve this pie warm with Roselani Tropics Hawaiian Vanilla Bean ice cream. Yum!

Raspberry Chocolate Truffle Cake

I often made this cake for Maui's own Dr. George Martin. Every time he planned a family event he would call my parents' restaurant, Hāliʻimaile General Store, and order this cake. And with each event, the size of the cake he ordered got bigger. The first cake was 10 inches; I think the last cake I made for them was a 16-inch round. That size cake can feed about 75 people!

There are three parts to this recipe: the luxurious chocolate cake, the truffle filling, and the soft chocolate glaze. We use fresh "made on Maui" products whenever possible. This recipe calls for Framboise de Maui Raspberry Wine from Maui's own Tedeschi Winery. If you can't find this in stores, you can substitute any raspberry liqueur, such as Chambord.

This rich cake is only for those willing to cast their dietary caution to the wind!

—Teresa Shurilla

CHOCOLATE CAKE
1¼ cup cake flour
½ cup cornstarch
1½ cup Dutch-process cocoa powder
2 teaspoons baking soda
2¼ cups sugar
4 large eggs
⅔ cup sour cream
⅔ cup vegetable oil
⅔ cup buttermilk
Fresh raspberries, if available

CHOCOLATE TRUFFLE FILLING
1 pound semi-sweet chocolate, broken or cut into chunks for ease of melting (always use the best chocolate you can buy; it's worth it)
½ cup Tedeschi Winery's Framboise de Maui Raspberry Wine
1¾ cups heavy cream

CHOCOLATE GLAZE
½ cup heavy cream
8 tablespoons (1 stick) unsalted butter
8 ounces bittersweet chocolate, chopped into small pieces (again, the best you can get)

TO PREPARE THE CAKE
Preheat the oven to 350 degrees. Grease and flour two 9-inch cake pans.

Sift together the flour, cornstarch, cocoa powder, and baking soda. In a separate bowl, whisk together the eggs, sour cream, and oil. Put the dry ingredients into the bowl of an electric mixer and then pour the egg mixture on top. Mix on medium speed for 3 minutes. Gradually add ⅓ of the buttermilk and mix another minute.

(recipe continued on page 158)

Continue in this fashion with the remaining buttermilk.

Pour the batter into the greased cake pans and bake for approximately 45 minutes, or until a cake tester inserted in the center of the cake comes out clean.

TO PREPARE THE CHOCOLATE TRUFFLE FILLING

Melt the chocolate in the top of a double boiler over medium heat. You can also melt it in the microwave if you are careful. Cook for 30 seconds at a time and stir after each pulse. Repeat until the chocolate is melted but not burned.

Over medium heat, in a separate saucepan, heat the Framboise; be careful not to let it boil. Add the melted chocolate to the Framboise and mix to combine. Set the mixture aside and let it cool down a little.

Whip the cream to the soft peak stage, or about 2–3 minutes in the bowl of an electric mixer on medium-high speed. Carefully fold the whipped cream into the warm chocolate.

TO PREPARE THE CHOCOLATE GLAZE

In a saucepan over medium-low heat, heat the cream and butter together until they are hot but not boiling. Put the chocolate into a large bowl and pour the cream and butter mixture over it. Stir until all ingredients have combined into a smooth mixture. Set aside.

When the cake is ready to glaze, you can reheat it in the microwave until it is liquid enough to pour over the cake. Be careful not to heat it up too much or the glaze will separate.

TO ASSEMBLE THE CAKE

Top one of the cake layers with truffle filling and sprinkle the filling with one or two baskets of fresh raspberries, if available. Place the second cake layer on top of the first; top the second layer with more truffle filling. Place the cake in the refrigerator to set, for 1–2 hours at a minimum. Cover the entire cake with the chocolate glaze and refrigerate again to set the glaze. Remove the cake from the refrigerator about ½ hour before serving.

Poached Pears with Yogurt Cream and Caramel Sauce

SERVES 6

In 1991, I prepared this recipe in a contest at the California Culinary Academy in San Francisco. This recipe won the grand prize: a three-week, all-expenses-paid trip to Vienna!

I have fond memories of the awards banquet, a stately affair held in the historic Banking Hall of the Old Federal Reserve Bank Building in downtown San Francisco. But of course the most incredible experience was the trip.

Visiting Vienna was amazing. I remember being scolded by a local female grower at the farmer's market for squeezing her tomatoes. Eating gelato while strolling along the shore of Lake Como was ultimately romantic. Also, drinking beer and eating large dill pickles at 7:00 am in the morning in Munich was astonishingly delicious and habit forming.

—Chris Speere

PUFF PASTRY "PEARS"
6 Pepperidge Farms Puff Pastry Squares, approximately 4 x 4-inch, frozen
1 egg
1 teaspoon milk

POACHING LIQUID FOR PEARS
2 cups Maui Brand Natural White Cane Sugar
3 cups water
1 sprig rosemary
1 teaspoon whole black peppercorns
3 Bartlett pears

CARAMEL SAUCE
1 cup Maui Brand Natural White Cane Sugar
$\frac{1}{2}$ cup water
$1\frac{1}{2}$ cups cream
4 tablespoons ($\frac{1}{2}$ stick) butter

YOGURT CREAM
2 cups whipping cream
$\frac{1}{4}$ cup plain yogurt

Powdered sugar
Raspberries
6 sprigs of rosemary

TO PREPARE THE PUFF PASTRY

Preheat the oven to 400 degrees. Lightly mist with water a 17 x 13-inch baking sheet. Place the frozen puff pastry squares on the baking sheet and cut them into 6 pear-shaped pieces.

Mix egg and milk in a small bowl and then brush lightly onto puff pastry pieces. Place the puff pastry in the oven and bake for 15 minutes, or until the puff pastry is a deep golden brown. It's easy to undercook the pastry, so be sure that your oven

(recipe continued on page 160)

is preheated to the full 400 degrees. The pastry is cooked if the bottom has turned golden brown, so peek at the bottom of one pastry before finally removing the sheet from the oven.

Remove the puff pastry from oven and let it cool for 3–4 minutes. Loosen the puff pastry from the baking sheet with a spatula. Using a sharp serrated knife, split the pear shaped puff pastries in half horizontally. Set aside until you are ready to assemble the dish.

TO POACH THE PEARS

Prepare the poaching liquid by mixing the sugar and water in a large saucepot. The sugar should be completely dissolved. Add the rosemary and peppercorns and bring to a boil. Reduce the heat and simmer for 30 minutes. Peel the pears, split them in half lengthwise, and remove the cores. Add the pears to the simmering poaching liquid and poach for approximately 12–15 minutes, or until the pears are easy to pierce with the tip of a sharp knife. Carefully remove the pears from the poaching liquid, and set them on an absorbent paper towel to drain and cool. Slice the pears vertically into 12 uniform pieces, being careful to keep the pear shape intact. Set aside the pears until it is time for the final assembly of the dessert.

TO PREPARE THE CARAMEL SAUCE

Melt the sugar in a large saucepot over medium heat; do not stir. Cook the sugar until it is golden brown and fully caramelized. This procedure should take 5–7 minutes. In a small bowl, combine the water and cream. Slowly and carefully add this cold mixture to the hot caramelized sugar, stirring as you pour a thin stream of liquid. Continue to simmer the caramel sauce, stirring occasionally, until the sauce is smooth and slightly thick. Remove the caramel sauce from the heat and stir in the butter. Keep the caramel sauce warm until you are ready to serve the dish.

TO PREPARE THE YOGURT CREAM

In a large stainless steel bowl, whip the cream until soft peaks are formed. Whisk in the yogurt and set aside.

TO ASSEMBLE THE DISH

Spoon ¼ cup of the caramel sauce onto a 6-inch plate. Place the bottom section of the pear-shaped puff pastry on top of the caramel sauce. Place one sliced pear on top of the pastry and press to fan out the pear slices. Cover the pear with ¼ cup of the yogurt cream and then replace the top section of the pear-shaped puff pastry. Repeat until all the desserts have been assembled. Garnish each plate with a dusting of powdered sugar, some fresh raspberries, and a small sprig of rosemary.

Dragon Fruit and Rambutan Sorbet

SERVES 4

When I was a student at the Maui Culinary Academy, we looked forward to student menu day in our Leis Family Class Act Restaurant. This dish was the highlight of one such menu day. I was proud to be part of the culinary team that created this dish. It features unusual flavors and a unique presentation: a fruit sorbet is served in a rambutan shell.

—*Kyle Kawakami*

---

1 cup peeled and cubed dragon fruit
2 rambutans, which should yield
    approximately 1 cup peeled and
    seeded rambutan pulp

1 can frozen guava juice (8-ounce size)
1 cup sugar
¼ cup lemon juice
4 sprigs fresh mint

TO PREPARE THE RAMBUTAN

Cut around the rambutan so that you have 2 approximately equal parts. Don't worry about the spikes; they're soft and won't hurt you. Pull the rambutan apart; inside, you'll find a ball of pulp with one large seed inside. Pop out the ball, then remove and discard the seed inside the ball. Cut up the pulp. Repeat with the second rambutan. Reserve the rambutan shells, which will be used as cups when the dessert is served.

TO PREPARE THE SORBET

In a food processor or blender with a puree function, combine the dragon fruit, rambutan, guava juice, sugar, and lemon juice. Process for 2 minutes or until all the ingredients are well puréed. Place the sorbet mixture in a large stainless steel bowl and freeze for ½ hour.

Using a fork (not a spoon, not a whisk, but a fork) stir the ice crystals around the edge of the bowl into the liquid center and return to the freezer. Continue to stir and freeze until the sorbet mixture resembles soft snow—this process should take approximately 1 hour.

TO SERVE

Use a small spoon to scoop the sorbet mixture into the rambutan shells. Garnish the sorbet with a fresh mint sprig and serve immediately.

If desired, serve the rest of the sorbet family-style on the side. The sorbet will also keep in the freezer in a tightly covered container for up to 1 month.

Heavenly Haupia Ice Cream Pie

Back when I created this pie, Mud Pies were common restaurant fare, especially at places like the Chart House, known for its "voluptuous servings." I decided I could improve on the Mud Pie by combining it with Grandpa's famous haupia ice cream recipe. Since I couldn't change anything in the ice cream (Grandpa stipulated that we must never alter or even add to his haupia ice cream recipe) I had to be creative in the other elements of the dessert. Thus this Heavenly Haupia Ice Cream Pie was born.

—Cathy Nobriga Kim

18 chocolate sandwich cookies, crushed	2 (12-ounce) jars of your favorite fudge topping, chilled
2 teaspoons butter, melted	Fresh berries (strawberries, raspberries, or both)
2 cartons Roselani Tropics Haupia ice cream (56 ounce size)	Sprigs of fresh mint (optional)

Temper the ice cream in your refrigerator for 30–45 minutes. This will allow it to warm slightly, and make it easier to whip.

Spray a 9 x 13-inch baking pan with pan release for ease of removal.

Mix the crushed cookies and the butter, in the pan or in a separate bowl. Pat the mixture evenly and firmly into the bottom of pan. Freeze for 30 minutes.

Put one carton of haupia ice cream into the bowl of an electric mixer and, using a whisk attachment, whip at low to medium speed until the ice cream is soft and smooth, about 10 minutes. Pour the softened ice cream onto the frozen crust. Now whip the second carton of ice cream the same way and add it to the pan as well. (If you have a large commercial mixer you might be able to do this all in one step.) Place a sheet of wax paper on top of the ice cream and freeze the pan for 6–8 hours.

Remove the pan from the freezer and take off the waxed paper. Smooth the fudge topping onto the ice cream in an even layer and return to the pan to the freezer for another 2–3 hours. To serve family-style at the table, garnish the whole pie with the berries and perhaps a few sprigs of mint. Or cut the pie into individual slices, plate, top with a sprig of fresh mint and sprinkle some berries on the plate. A chilled plate works best.

Gingered Coconut and Maui Gold Pineapple Tapioca

SERVES 8

Tapioca pudding is one of my comfort foods. It brings back fond memories of lazy childhood summers. In this island-style recipe, the hot and spicy flavor of ginger blends perfectly with the sweetness of Maui Gold pineapple.

The Maui Roasted Pineapple Jam is available for purchase at the Maui Culinary Academy and at gourmet shops throughout the islands. You can purchase small pearl tapioca from any well-stocked Asian grocery store or buy it online.

—*Teresa Shurilla*

1½ cups heavy cream	1 cup small pearl tapioca
1 cup unsweetened coconut milk	4 cups water, for tapioca
½ cup Maui Brand Natural White Cane Sugar	8 tablespoons Maui Roasted Pineapple Jam
2 teaspoons grated fresh ginger	Whipped cream
6 egg yolks	Mint sprigs
1 teaspoon pure vanilla extract	Thin wedges of Maui Gold pineapple

Place the cream, coconut milk, sugar, vanilla, and ginger in a stainless steel saucepan. Mix well, then bring the cream mixture to a simmer over medium heat. Put the egg yolks into a stainless steel bowl and whisk gently for 1 minute. Pour the cream mixture over the yolks while continuing to whisk. Return the cream and egg mixture to the stainless steel saucepan. Cook the cream and egg mixture over low heat for three minutes, stirring gently and constantly, or until the mixture begins to thicken slightly. Be careful not to overcook the egg and cream mixture. Strain the mixture into a clean stainless steel bowl and immediately cool over an ice bath which is a larger bowl filled with ice and a little water. When cool, the cream and egg mixture should be thick enough to coat the back of a spoon. Once it has cooled to room temperature, it should be refrigerated.

Bring the 4 cups of water to a boil. Stir the tapioca into the boiling water and cook until each pearl is opaque. Gently mix the cooked tapioca into the cooled cream mixture.

Place 1 tablespoon of Maui Roasted Pineapple Jam into the bottom of a clear martini glass. Ladle tapioca cream mixture on top of the jam, and refrigerate immediately.

Serve the tapioca pudding completely chilled with freshly whipped cream, a sprig of mint, and a thin wedge of Maui Gold pineapple.

Pineapple Fritters with Roselani Mango 'n Cream Ice Cream and Coconut Tuiles

SERVES 6

Maui Culinary Academy has had a long and friendly relationship with the Maui Pineapple Company. On several occasions the company has asked me to come up with tasty new dishes using their incredibly sweet, low-acid Maui Gold pineapple. This is my all-time favorite pineapple creation.

I suggest you make the tuiles first and then the fritters, because these fritters are best served right from the fryer.

This dessert goes perfectly with the Mango Purée (see page 22) and Raspberry Coulis (see page 22), and makes a colorful presentation.

—Teresa Shurilla

COCONUT TUILES
1 cup powdered sugar
2 eggs, beaten
1 cup dried unsweetened coconut or macaroon powder
1½ tablespoons unsalted butter, melted

1 cup fine panko (Japanese-style bread crumbs)
3 cups canola oil
1 cup Maui Brand Natural White Cane Sugar
1 tablespoon cinnamon

PINEAPPLE FRITTERS
1 medium Maui Gold pineapple
¼ cup all-purpose flour
2 eggs, beaten lightly

Mint leaves
Raspberry Coulis (see page 22)
Mango Purée (see page 22)
Roselani Mango 'n Cream ice cream

TO PREPARE THE TUILES

Mix all the ingredients together and refrigerate overnight.

Scoop 1 tablespoon of the mixture onto a cookie sheet that is lined with a non-stick silpat or heavily greased baking paper. Dip a fork in cold water and press down on the cookie dough, spreading it out to form a 3-inch circle. Repeat until you have 4 or fewer circles of dough on the sheet.

Bake at 325 degrees for 12–15 minutes, or until lightly golden around the edges. Immediately roll the tuiles into a cone shape and let them cool. I do only a few at a time because they harden quickly; 4 is the most I can do before the tuiles become too hard to roll.

Repeat this process until all the dough is baked.

TO PREPARE THE FRITTERS

Peel the pineapple, removing the eyes, and slice into 6–8 rings, ½-inch or less in thickness. Remove the core with an apple corer.

Dip each slice, first in the flour, then in the egg and finally in the panko flakes. Heat the oil to 365 degrees and begin to fry the pineapple slices one by one. Fry until golden brown, approximately 4–5 minutes per side.

Combine sugar and cinnamon in a bowl. Immediately after removing the fritters from the oil, dip into the sugar and cinnamon mix to lightly coat.

TO SERVE

Place ¼ cup of the mango puree on a plate. Place a warm pineapple fritter on top of the puree, then top with Roselani Mango 'n Cream ice cream and a coconut tuile. The cone of tuile can be placed into the hole in the center of the pineapple and filled with the ice cream. Garnish with mint. To finish, drizzle raspberry coulis on top of the mango puree.

Roselani Tropics Shaka Shake

This recipe came from an old friend who operated an ice cream parlor in the 1980s. She was a spunky woman who resembled the outrageous comedienne Phyllis Diller in many ways. My friend "spiced up" her afternoons with these shakes while watching the sunset from her lanai on Maui's south side. Cheers, old friend.

To add some "spice," add 1–2 ounces of your favorite spirits to the shake. Rum and champagne work particularly well with this recipe!

—*Cathy Nobriga Kim*

1½ cups (3 scoops) Roselani Tropics Pa'uwela Sunrise Ice Cream

1 cup (2 scoops) Roselani Tropics Haupia Ice Cream
¾ cup pineapple juice, chilled

Temper (allow to warm slightly) the ice cream in your refrigerator for 20 minutes. Scoop into a blender. Add the chilled juice. Blend the shake on high speed for 15–20 seconds or until it is completely mixed and thoroughly smooth. Serve the shakes in your best glasses.

Tuaca-Orange Crème Brûlée

SERVES 8–10

Classic crème brûlée usually "outsells" any flavored version. This recipe is an exception; it has always been very popular. It marries orange-flavored liqueur with rich custard and caramelized sugar.

—Stanton Ho

3 cups heavy cream	Pinch salt
1 cup milk	9 egg yolks
1 vanilla bean	3 tablespoons Tuaca (or other orange-flavored liqueur)
½ teaspoon finely grated orange zest	
¾ cups + 2 tablespoons Maui Brand Natural White Cane Sugar	1 teaspoon pure vanilla extract

In a saucepot, combine the cream, the milk, vanilla bean, and orange zest. Bring this mixture to a boil.

In a mixing bowl, combine the ¾ cup sugar, salt, yolks, liqueur and vanilla extract. Mix well.

Temper this mixture with the hot cream mixture. Tempering is mixing a little of the hot mixture into the cold, stirring constantly to prevent "scrambled eggs." After you have mixed ⅓ of the hot into the cold, you can then mix the cold into the hot. This helps to combine the egg yolks smoothly. Cook over low heat for 5 minutes. Strain the mixture through a fine strainer.

Preheat the oven to 325 degrees. Place an ovenproof shallow soufflé or tart dish into a bain marie—a roasting pan filled with enough water to reach about ⅓ of the way up the soufflé dish. Pour the prepared mix into the soufflé dish. Cook for 45 minutes or until the mixture is set; it will have the consistency of jello fresh out of the fridge. Allow to cool before refrigerating.

Before serving, cover the top with the remaining sugar and caramelize either with a kitchen propane torch or by placing the dish under the broiler for no more than 3 minutes. Be very careful not to burn the sugar.

Coconut Flan with Mini Churros

I love flan. I like the way the caramelized sugar runs over the top when it is inverted. I added a tropical twist with coconut milk and Coco Lopez™. We served this dessert in our Leis Family Class Act Restaurant, pairing it with mini churros made with éclair paste.

—*Teresa Shurilla*

COCONUT FLAN
4 cups milk
1 cup coconut milk
6 tablespoons Coco Lopez™ or cream of coconut
¾ cup Maui Brand Natural White Cane Sugar
6 egg yolks
6 whole eggs
1½ teaspoons coconut extract

CARAMEL
2 cups Maui Brand Natural White Cane Sugar
½ cup water

MINI CHURROS
½ recipe éclair paste (see page 172)
1 cup Maui Brand Natural White Cane Sugar
2 teaspoons cinnamon
2 cups canola oil

TO PREPARE THE FLAN

In a medium saucepan, bring the milk, coconut milk, Coco Lopez, and ¾ cup of sugar to a boil. Put the egg yolks, eggs, and coconut extract in a mixing bowl and mix well. Slowly pour the hot liquid into the eggs, mixing or whisking constantly. You can use an electric mixer or a hand whisk. If you don't do this slowly and carefully, the eggs will curdle and the flan will be lumpy.

TO PREPARE THE CARAMEL

Mix the water and sugar in a shallow saucepan and cook over medium heat until the caramel turns a medium amber color, or about 10 minutes. Make sure the sides of the pot are completely clean. Do not stir the caramel; rather, wash down any liquid that gets onto the sides of the pot with a wet pastry brush.

TO BAKE THE FLAN

Carefully divide the caramel evenly among 6 oven-proof dishes, custard cups, or ramekins. (I use white ceramic 10-ounce soufflé dishes.) Pour the caramel over the bottom of the dishes and let it cool and harden. After it has hardened, pour the flan mix over the caramel, taking care to evenly divide between the dishes.

Place the dishes in a roasting pan and fill with water until it is halfway up the outside of the dishes. This creates a water bath, or bain marie (see page 179 for tips). Place the bain marie into a 325-degree oven for 60-75 minutes. Before you remove the pan from the oven, test to see if the flan has set. Shake the pan; if the surface of the flan has solidified and jiggles only slightly, the flan is done and will continue to set as it cools. It is best to make the flan the day before serving. This gives it a long time to cool and set, and makes it easier to unmold.

To unmold, dip the bottom of the custard cup in hot water. Run a knife around the outside edge of the flan, then turn it upside down over a serving plate. You may have to give it a little shake to loosen it.

TO PREPARE THE CHURROS

Combine the sugar and cinnamon and set aside.

Put the 2 cups of canola oil in a heavy pot and heat to 365 degrees. Cut some parchment baking paper into 3 x 3-inch squares and spray the squares with a non-stick spray. Pipe the éclairs with a plain pastry tip onto the baking paper. The lines of éclair paste should be about 2 inches in length. You can fit 2 onto 1 baking paper.

Carefully lower the éclair paste into the hot oil, one sheet at a time, allowing the éclairs to slide off the paper into the oil. When the churros start to brown, or about 7 minutes, remove them from the oil and roll them in the cinnamon sugar.

TO SERVE

Nestle two or three churros against each flan and serve immediately.

Lemongrass Crème Brûlée

After a working stint on the Mainland, I returned to Maui and found I was using more Asian flavors in my pastry. We have served this dessert several times in our Leis Family Class Act Restaurant and it always gets compliments. I usually serve this with some kind of biscuit or cookie. They go wonderfully with the Lemon Macadamia Nut Biscotti on page 150.

—*Teresa Shurilla*

---

1 quart heavy cream
1 cup + 6 tablespoons Maui Brand
   Natural White Cane Sugar
1 tablespoon peeled and chopped
   fresh ginger

2 stalks lemongrass
12 egg yolks
6 custard cups or soufflé dishes
   (10-ounce size)

TO PREPARE THE CRÈME BRÛLÉE

Wash and crush the bulb ends of the lemongrass stalks.

Place the cream, 1 cup of the sugar, the whole lemongrass stalks, and ginger, into a stainless steel saucepan. I prefer to use stainless steel, because aluminum tends to give the custard a grayish tint. Once the mix begins to boil, turn it off and let it steep for approximately 20 minutes.

Turn on the heat again. Just before the mixture starts to boil again, remove it from the heat and pour it in a slow stream over the unbeaten yolks, whisking all the while.

Strain the entire mixture through a fine mesh strainer, being careful to push all the mix through—including the lemongrass, which should be very soft now.

Place the custard cups into a baking dish which can serve as a water bath, or bain marie (see page 179 for tips). Pour the lemongrass-cream mixture into the cups, and then fill the baking dish halfway up the sides of the cups with hot water. Carefully place the bain marie into the oven at 300 degrees. Cook for 60–75 minutes, or until custard jiggles only slightly. Remove the pan from the oven and let the cups cool in the water bath. Refrigerate 4–5 hours at a minimum and preferably overnight.

TO CARAMELIZE THE SUGAR

You will need either a kitchen propane torch or a broiler for the next step. Use the back of a spoon to spread 1 tablespoon of the sugar on each brûlée. If you are using a kitchen propane torch, fan it lightly over the surface of the custard to caramelize the sugar. Caramelized sugar is golden-brown; don't let it get any darker than that or you will burn the sugar. If you don't have a torch, you can put the cups under the broiler for approximately 2 minutes; again, you must watch closely so that the sugar doesn't burn.

TO SERVE

I like to serve this crème brûlée with a few slices of my Lemon Macadamia Nut Biscotti (see page 150). However, you can use any biscotti or crisp cookie as a garnish. The contrast of smooth and crisp is delightful.

Chocolate Éclairs
with Vanilla Bean Custard

When I began working in pastry, pâte à choux—or éclair paste, as it is also known—was one of the first things that I learned to make. In this recipe, I use milk rather water; the milk makes the paste drier and sturdier when it is cooked. Whenever we serve these éclairs in the Pā'ina Food Court, they always sell out.

—*Teresa Shurilla*

ÉCLAIR PASTE
1 cup water
8 tablespoons (1 stick) unsalted butter
3/4 teaspoon salt
1 cup + 2 tablespoons all-purpose flour
4 eggs

VANILLA BEAN CUSTARD
1 1/2 cups whole milk
1/2 vanilla bean or 2 teaspoons vanilla
    extract

8 egg yolks
3/4 cups sugar
1/3 cup cornstarch
1 tablespoon unsalted butter

CHOCOLATE GANACHE
1/2 cup chopped semi-sweet chocolate
1/2 cup heavy cream

TO PREPARE THE ÉCLAIRS

In a thick bottomed saucepan, bring the water, butter, and salt to a rapid boil. Remove the mixture from the heat and add all of the flour at once, all the while stirring vigorously using a wooden spoon or tempered spatula. Place the saucepan back on medium heat and cook until the paste is thick and pulls away from the side of the pan. Pour the paste into a mixing bowl and stir it with a wooden spoon; this removes a bit of the heat. Add the eggs one by one, stirring after each addition. Using a plain pastry tip # 808, or one that has an opening as big as a dime, pipe 4-inch lines of paste onto a cookie sheet lined with parchment baking paper. Bake at 400 degrees for 25–30 minutes or until the éclairs are golden brown. Let them cool while you are making the custard.

TO PREPARE THE CUSTARD

Put the milk in a stainless steel or enameled cast iron pot (aluminum or uncoated cast iron will stain the custard). Start to bring the milk to a boil. If you are using a vanilla bean, slice it down the middle and scrape out the seeds. Put both the bean and the scrapings into the milk. If you are using vanilla extract, add it at the end of the cooking process.

Separate the eggs. Place the egg yolks in a bowl and whisk the sugar into the eggs, adding the sugar gradually rather than all at once. Whip the yolks and sugar together until the mixture turns a pale yellow. Sift in the cornstarch and mix well.

Add half of the hot milk to the egg yolk mixture, adding it slowly and gradually as you whisk. If you add it too quickly, the eggs may curdle. When the eggs and half the milk are well-mixed, pour the mixture back into the pot with the rest of the milk, mix, and bring to a boil. Boil on medium heat for 3–5 minutes, stirring occasionally and watching that the mixture doesn't stick to the sides or bottom of the pot.

Remove the pot from the heat and stir in the vanilla extract and the butter. If you used a vanilla bean, be sure to remove the pod. Pour the custard into a container and cover it with plastic wrap. The wrap should touch the surface of the custard, so that the custard doesn't form a skin. Let it cool in the refrigerator for at least 1 hour.

TO PREPARE THE GANACHE
Put the chopped chocolate in a bowl. Bring the cream to a boil; pour the hot cream over the chocolate. Stir until all the chocolate is melted.

TO ASSEMBLE
Poke 2 holes in the bottom of each éclair shell, one at each end. Using a pastry bag, fill the éclairs with the custard and then dip the filled éclairs in the glaze. Cool the éclairs in the fridge until the chocolate is set, which should take about 20–30 minutes.

TIPS AND TECHNIQUES

MAKING CRACKED PEPPER

If you want pepper that's cracked rather than ground, you can improvise with a sauté pan. Spread whole peppercorns evenly on a hard surface and then rock a sauté pan over them. Hold the rim of the pan with one hand and the handle with the other and rock until you hear the peppercorns cracking.

You can also pulse them for a few seconds in a clean coffee grinder. Just be careful not to pulse too long, or you'll have ground rather than cracked pepper.

TOASTING SPICES, NUTS, AND COCONUT

A few recipes call for toasted spices, sesame seeds, nuts, or coconut. Toasting brings out the flavor and adds more fragrance to the finished dish.

TO TOAST SPICES AND SEEDS

Heat a heavy skillet over medium heat. Add whole spices or seeds to dry pan and stir frequently, until fragrant, warmed, and slightly darker, about 3 to 5 minutes. Some whole spices, such as cumin, mustard and fennel, will pop. Remove from heat and let cool.

TO TOAST NUTS OR COCONUT

Preheat oven to 325 degrees. Spread nuts or shredded coconut evenly on an ungreased baking pan. Place pan in oven for 5–10 minutes or until the nuts or coconut are golden brown. Stir once or twice during the process to toast evenly and prevent burning. Remove from heat and let cool.

HOW TO PEEL TOMATOES

A peeled tomato blends better in sauces, and it's quite easy to do. First, you'll need to blanch the tomatoes. Bring 2 quarts of salted water to a boil in a large pot. Using a sharp paring knife, cut an "x" on the bottom of each whole tomato. Drop the tomatoes into the boiling water and cook them for a scant 8 seconds. Using a slotted spoon, quickly remove the tomatoes and plunge them into a bowl of ice water, which stops them from cooking further. The skin should now come off very easily. Use your hands or a sharp paring knife to remove the skin.

ALL ABOUT KNIVES

KNIFE SKILLS

Professional chefs spend a good deal of their life cutting up food. They buy good knives, sharpen them frequently, and store them properly. They learn how to cut precisely, quickly, and safely. Knife skills are a large part of a professional chef's training.

Two cuts that you'll see in many of the recipes here include julienne and chiffonade.

- ❧ To **julienne**, cut the food into square slivers like wooden matchsticks. First, cut the food into thin slices, then cut the slices into strips.
- ❧ To **chiffonade**, which is a popular cut for leafy herbs such as basil, first pick the leaves off the stem. For a basil chiffonade, stack up the leaves, then roll the stack into a cylinder. Cut extremely thin slices across the cylinder, forming thin, long shreds of basil.

HOW TO BUY KNIVES

If you care enough about cooking to buy a serious cookbook like this one, it is likely that you have already invested some money in a good kitchen knife or knives. If you haven't, go to a kitchen store and check out their knife collections. You aren't looking for the most expensive knife: you will be looking for knives that feel right in your hand. You don't need to buy a whole set of knives. Two general purpose cook's knives, short (3–4 inches) and medium (8–9 inches), will take care of most of your chopping.

KNIFE CARE

Once you have a good knife, you need to take care of it. Sharpen it as often as necessary to keep it razor sharp. A dull knife is dangerous. You have to push it through food forcefully, which means that you're more likely to hurt yourself if the knife slips.

OTHER CUTTING TOOLS

Restaurant chefs preparing large quantities of food use specialized tools such as mandolins and food processors. A mandolin is the traditional tool; it's a manual slicer/shredder. You may want to buy either or both of these tools. However, you may also find that when you just have one or two onions to chop, it's often quicker to use a knife than it is to set up and then wash the mandolin or food processor.

CORNSTARCH SLURRY, ROUX, AND BEURRE MANIÉ

CORNSTARCH SLURRY

Many Asian dishes feature sauces thickened with a cornstarch slurry. To make a slurry, mix about a tablespoon of cornstarch and 2 tablespoons cold water in a small bowl (or use the proportions your recipe recommends). Make sure there are no lumps. Then stir the slurry into warm sauce or pan juices. If you try to add the cornstarch directly to the hot liquid, it will clump. Hence the importance of mixing it with cold water first.

Some cooks substitute powdered arrowroot for cornstarch. They claim arrowroot gives a cleaner, clearer taste than cornstarch. Arrowroot is also kosher for Passover, which cornstarch is not.

ROUX

A roux is a thickener made with flour cooked in butter, oil, pan juices, or some other fat. The cook melts the fat in a sauté pan or small saucepot over medium heat, then adds an equal amount of all-purpose flour. The cook whisks the flour into the melted fat to form a smooth paste. Then liquid is added, slowly, whisking all the while, so that no lumps form. The roux can then be added to a hot soup, or used to make gravy or sauce.

If the roux is cooked until the flour darkens, it becomes blond, brown, or dark brown roux. It develops a stronger "toasted" flavor, but loses some of its thickening power.

Classic French cooking made great use of roux. In recent years, there has been a strong reaction against roux-based sauces and gravies. Modern cooks are more likely to reduce sauces or pan juices, by cooking them until water evaporates and the sauce thickens.

BEURRE MANIÉ

Beurre manié is made by kneading together equal parts soft butter and flour. Restaurant cooks will make a log of beurre manié beforehand and store it in the refrigerator. If a soup or sauce needs thickening pronto, and there is no time to make a roux, a pinch of beurre manié, dropped into hot liquid and stirred vigorously, will do the trick.

SWEATING, SAUTÉING, SEARING, BLANCHING, AND DEGLAZING

SWEAT
To sweat a food is to cook it in a small amount of fat, usually covered, over low heat without browning until the food softens and releases moisture. This is typically done with vegetables.

SAUTÉ
To sauté is to cook a food quickly in a hot pan using a small amount of fat.

SEAR
To sear is to cook a food, usually meat, fish or shellfish, in a shallow pan over high heat utilizing little fat. This cooking method develops a flavorful brown crust that holds in the juices of the meat or seafood.

It is important to sear in a pan large enough to hold the meat or seafood without crowding, or the steam created will not be able to escape the pan, and excess moisture will hinder the browning process. If necessary, cook the meat or seafood in several batches.

BLANCH
To blanch a food is to cook it for a short amount of time in boiling water, usually no more than 1-2 minutes. After removing the food from the boiling water, it is quickly placed in ice water, which "shocks" the food and stops it from cooking. This technique is frequently done with vegetables and fruits. Blanching also preserves the color and flavor of the food, keeps it crisp, and also preserves the vitamin content.

DEGLAZE
To deglaze is to add some liquid, such as wine or stock, to a pan you have used to sauté or sear a food. The liquid will dissolve the juices crusted on the bottom of the pan. Be sure to stir or whisk thoroughly.

DEEP FRYING
A fair number of the recipes in this book ask you to deep fry ingredients. All the deep-fried dishes will require a large pot, large quantities of cooking oil, a frying thermometer, a skimmer, tongs or a large deep frying basket, and paper or cloth towels for draining the fried foods. Follow these tips for the best results.

OIL
Whatever oil you use, you should know its smokepoint: the heat, in degrees, at which it starts to smoke and break down. You must keep your oil below its smokepoint.

Smokepoints for common deep frying oils are: butter (350 degrees Fahrenheit); lard (361 to 401); vegetable shortening (356 to 370); olive oil (about 375); canola, corn, grapeseed, peanut, and safflower oils (441 to 450). An unrefined oil typically has a lower smokepoint than a highly refined oil.

Every time you use oil for frying, you lower its smokepoint. Many chefs will use frying oil only three times. After that, the smoke point is too low for successful frying.

For that reason, you should never mix used oil with new oil. When you finish frying and the oil has cooled, you should strain the oil through cheesecloth or a coffee filter, to remove any burnt particles, store the oil in a closed container, and label it as to how many times and when it was last used. It should be stored in a cool dark place, or even in the refrigerator. Refrigerated oil may get cloudy, but the cloudiness clears after the oil warms to room temperature.

What should you do with the used oil? Here at the Academy, we make sure that our used oil goes to local companies that turn it into biodiesel, for auto fuel. As a home cook, you probably produce an extremely low volume of used oil, and may have a hard time finding anyone to recycle it. Still, there's no harm in putting out the word, over the coconut wireless or on Craigslist, offering to donate the oil to recyclers.

FRYING THERMOMETER
Now that you know about smokepoint, you understand why it's important to use a frying thermometer. You need to keep the oil hot enough to fry, but below its smokepoint.

The correct temperature is also crucial for making delicious fried food. If the oil is too cool, the food will take too long to cook and oil will soak into the food, making it greasy and indigestible. If the oil is too hot, it will burn the outside of the food before the inside is cooked. The recipes here detail the correct temperature for deep frying that particular food.

Be careful when you add food to the oil. If you add too much at once, the temperature of the oil will drop and your food won't cook properly.

SKIMMER
Fried foods may leave particles of batter or food behind in the oil. You need to skim these out as you cook so that they don't contaminate the oil. Japanese cooks call the little blobs of cooked tempura batter agedama, and use them as garnish.

TONGS, LONG COOKING CHOPSTICKS, OR A DEEP FRYING BASKET

Unless you have asbestos fingers, you'll need something to put the food into the oil and take it out again.

TOWELS FOR DRAINING

When the food is fried, take it out of the oil and put it on a cloth or paper towel. You'll probably want to put the towel on a plate or sheet pan, just to keep oil off your counter. The towel absorbs any excess oil.

BATTER FOR DEEP FRYING

Several of our recipes call for the food to be coated in batter before it is fried. Follow these batter-making tips for the best results:

- Mix the batter with a few swift strokes, so that you do not develop the low level of gluten in the flour.

- Use low-gluten flours, like all-purpose or cake flour, or even rice flour.

Gluten is the protein in wheat flour. When you are making bread, you want to develop the gluten by kneading it. It forms long stretchy chains that give the bread its rise and structure. But when you are deep frying, you want to avoid long chains of gluten, which will make the batter coating tough.

BAIN MARIE

Several of the crème brûlée or flan recipes direct you to put the egg mixture into individual ramekins or small ceramic pots, then bake them in a bain marie, or water bath.

A bain marie is simply a large pan filled with water. To follow this cooking method, place the crème brûlée- or flan-filled ramekins into the large pan. The water should reach at least $\frac{1}{2}$ or $\frac{3}{4}$ of the way up the sides of the ramekins. You do not need to cover the pan with foil. You are not trying to steam the crèmes or the flans. The purpose of the water is to keep the temperature of the ramekins below the boiling point of water. Even if the oven is 350 degrees, the egg mixture in the ramekins will remain below 212 degrees. If you cook the crèmes or flans at a higher temperature, the egg proteins will coagulate and lump. You will end up with scrambled eggs rather than a smooth, creamy custard.

MAUI CULINARY ACADEMY

ABOUT THE MAUI CULINARY ACADEMY

MISSION AND VISION

Maui Culinary Academy at Maui Community College envisions itself as a world-class culinary arts training center for the state of Hawai'i. Founded in 1972, our culinary arts program seeks to draw and train students from Maui, across the state, and the rest of the country and world. Our Academy is like no other culinary arts program in the nation. A sense of "Aloha" lives in all we do and accomplish with our students, who come from different ethnic and cultural backgrounds. Given this rich diversity, creating a sense of place and community continues to be one of the most important aspects of our teaching environment, and a key component in our students' educational and career success.

Our new $17 million dollar Pā'ina training facility provides instruction leading towards three degree options including an AAS in Culinary Arts, AAS in Baking, and an AAS in Restaurant Supervision. The Pā'ina facility serves as a total work-based learning center, where students learn and model the best practices of the food service industry. Students gain hands-on training and prepare for the real world by operating a full-service restaurant—The Leis Family Class Act Restaurant—and six fast casual food outlets in the spacious Pā'ina Food Court. The Academy also offers specialized certificate-training programs for professionals, in addition to professional development classes with visiting distinguished chefs. Our graduates work in leading restaurants in Hawai'i, Napa Valley, Las Vegas, Colorado, Oregon and Washington. Many graduates are now successful entrepreneurs and highly acclaimed chefs.

Chef Instructor Tom Lelli teaches students the finer points of meat butchery.

Our culinary arts program is continually evolving. With a goal to educate and support our future chefs and culinary professionals, our instructors and staff have been recognized for exemplary efforts in the following areas:

COMMUNITY PARTNERSHIPS

Maui Culinary Academy has long history of working with local groups and organizations and also the restaurant and hospitality industry to improve our community. Tours, demonstrations, and luncheons are provided to seniors, family organizations, rotary clubs, youth agencies, and local schools. Students volunteer at numerous Maui food and wine events including Taste of Lahaina, Kapalua Food and Wine Festival, and Maui Arts & Cultural Center's Maui Calls, and work alongside our faculty to present food offerings, conduct cooking demonstrations, or provide outreach to future students. We also work closely with *Maui No Ka 'Oi* magazine to host the annual 'Aipono Awards, which celebrates the best of Maui's restaurants and chefs. Proceeds from many community events, including our annual Noble Grape fundraising dinner, go back to the Academy to support our programs. These numerous community partnerships have provided the Academy much visibility and support, and have helped to earn pride and respect for our program from our peers, students, and Maui's visitors and residents.

Academy faculty with guest chefs at a recent Noble Grape fundraising dinner.

ENVIRONMENTAL AND ECOLOGICAL SUSTAINABILITY

At the Academy, "going green" is not just a buzzword, it is a way of life. Our innovative environmental approach to our classroom instruction and also our business operations has set the standards for the entire college campus and serves as a model of sustainability to the Maui community. We are committed to building a sustainable culture in all facets of our program—from farm to table. These initiatives include:

- Supporting small and large-scale local farmers, and showcasing their produce and products in our kitchens and menu offerings.

- Eliminating the use of trans-fats throughout our recipe development and food preparation.

- Maintaining a highly visible herb garden on campus and hydroponics gardens in our kitchen labs to utilize in our teachings and in recipe creation.

- Implementing a composting program where students learn and practice separating compostable matter in our kitchens labs, allowing us to provide kitchen green waste to local farmers.

- Eliminating polypropylene containers and plastic bags in the Pā'ina Food Court and culinary arts facility, while utilizing biodegradable containers and beverage cups.

- Using sustainable, recyclable products in our food outlets.

- Recycling all our glass, plastic, and cardboard food and beverage containers.

- Initiating the use of recyclable and reusable bags on campus.

We want to encourage our graduates to lead similar initiatives in their culinary careers. Our goal is to serve as a catalyst for change, to help motivate and encourage even greater efforts toward environmental sustainability on our campus and our island.

Culinary students preparing for lunch service at our Leis Family Class Act Restaurant.

INNOVATIVE RESEARCH AND DEVELOPMENT

Our well-equipped Research and Development Center is the only one of its kind in Hawai'i. It is a place where students, entrepreneurs, and local agribusiness can work to develop new and value-added food products. Through the Center, our students gain hands-on skills in food manufacturing, processing control, marketing, sales and business management, which helps them become more marketable in their professional endeavors. This enhances our workforce and ultimately benefits the community.

Through the Center, our students have produced a successful line of Maui-made gourmet products such as Raspberry Wine Jelly, Roasted Pineapple Jam, Mochachino Scone Mix, Thai Basil Sea Salt, 100% Maui Coffee, Mango and Vanilla Macadamia Nut Sugars, a Sugar-Free Oat Cake, and Maui Coffee Spice Rub. The products are available for purchase through the Academy, at gourmet shops throughout Hawai'i, and increasingly around the country. Sales of our products benefit the Academy and help support the long-term sustainability of our program as a self-managing, profit generating entity.

The Academy's Maui-made gourmet food products.

ABOUT THE COOKBOOK

No culinary school would be complete without its own cookbook, and *Taste of Maui* showcases the very best of our island's cooking from our chef-instructors and friends of the program. Our dedicated faculty is the key ingredient behind the success of our award-winning culinary arts program. Their in-depth knowledge and teaching experience, their outstanding culinary skills, and their deep ties to the Maui community truly make the Maui Culinary Academy what it is: unique, high-quality, and accessible to all.

We truly hope you enjoy this recipe collection. From our Academy's kitchens to yours, thank you for joining us in the celebration of taste: A Taste of Maui!

Chris Speere
Program Coordinator
Maui Culinary Academy

For more information on our program, or to purchase our student-created gourmet food products, visit us at www.mauiculinary.com.

KOMO MAI E 'AI

Come and eat, all are welcome! Maui Culinary Academy invites you to experience a variety of unique cuisines in the dynamic learning environment of our critically-acclaimed Pā'ina Food Court. Fine dining is available upstairs at the elegant Leis Family Class Act Restaurant, recently voted the Best Business Lunch by *Maui No Ka 'Oi* magazine.

PĀ'INA FOOD COURT (Open Monday-Friday)

Farm to Table	offers locally grown foods
World Plate	sells Maui ethnic and international cuisines
PANIOLO GRILL	serves up hearty comfort food with a trendy twist
Raw Fish Camp	offers fresh sushi made-to-order
CAMPUS CAFE	dishes up lunchtime favorite
The Patisserie	has something to satisfy every sweet tooth

THE LEIS FAMILY CLASS ACT RESTAURANT

Class Act

Reservations (808) 984-3280
4-course prix fixe lunch,
Wednesdays and Fridays

Maui Culinary Academy
Pā'ina Building • Maui Community College
310 West Ka'ahumanu Avenue • Kahului, Hawai'i 96732 • (808) 984-32

Staff (pictured left to right): **Tom Lelli, Teresa Shurilla, Kyle Kawakami, Dean Louie, Chris Speere, Ben Marquez, Robert Santos**

CONTRIBUTORS

MAUI CULINARY ACADEMY CHEF INSTRUCTORS

A local boy from Hāliʻimaile, Maui, Chef Instructor (Assistant Professor) **DARRYL DELA CRUZ** taught at the Maui Culinary Academy for 14 years before relocating to the Mainland with his family in July 2007. He was a major influence on the program at Maui Community College. Chef Darryl contributed many recipes to this book, most of them from his beloved Paniolo Grill station in the Pāʻina Food Court. Here's his fondest childhood cooking memory:

> "When I was about 12 years old, I made a 'sardine' sandwich from a recipe in the 1960s edition of the Culinary Institute of America Cookbook for my younger sister. She thought that was the best meal she had ever eaten!"

Chef **KYLE KAWAKAMI** is a 2003 program graduate, and is the newest faculty member at the Maui Culinary Academy. He says:

> "As an alumni, the Maui Culinary Academy has provided me with an excellent culinary education as well as outstanding professional opportunities."

He shares this childhood memory: "I recall a family vacation to New York City when I was about 10 years old. We walked into Zabar's and I was amazed at the variety of foods available. The sights, sounds and smells of the food being cooked in the street carts in New York really spurred my interest in the culinary arts."

Chef Instructor **THOMAS LELLI** is a well-known name and face on Maui. Before joining the MCA faculty he showcased his considerable culinary skills at Hāliʻimaile General Store and Mañana Garage. This talented East Coast native remembers:

> "...actually thinking it was worth suffering through church and Sunday school because I knew after we would go to my grandmother's house. That was like going

to Neverland, with the aromas of fresh baked fruit pies on the windowsill, a slow cooking roast in the oven, and simmering escarole soup on the stove. I would help her make homemade tortellini and for my efforts I would get to taste everything before everybody else, just like a chef does."

Once a budding chef, now a real chef and chef instructor, Tom Lelli has managed the Leis Family Class Act Restaurant for the last four years. He is a demanding but popular instructor.

Chef Instructor **DEAN LOUIE** came to the Maui Culinary Academy in 2001. He brought with him a wealth of restaurant experience. He has worked in luxury hotels, private catering, international resorts and, most recently, successful restaurant ventures in both Guam and on Maui where he was both chef and owner. He is determined to give his students the basic skills they'll need to succeed in the professional kitchen.

Chef Dean was raised in San Francisco and Hawai'i. He is proud of his Chinese-American heritage, which he feels has given him a strong culinary foundation. His first teachers were his parents, who taught him to cook carefully and share generously. His personal credo: "I value the connection between good cooking and well-being and try to emphasize that in my teaching and personal life."

After graduating from the Maui Culinary Academy in 1990, Maui native and upcountry boy **BEN MARQUEZ** went on excel at such prestigious venues as the Hyatt Regency Maui. The pull of his alma mater was strong; he was often invited to help out with special events and catering jobs. Finally, in 1999, he returned full time and has been Chef Instructor Ben Marquez

ever since. He is the past president of the ACF Maui Chefs and Cooks Association. He believes that the Maui Culinary Academy "sets the standard for culinary training in the State of Hawai'i."

Chef Instructor **ROBERT SANTOS** has been a dedicated member of the MCA faculty for 28 years. This Olowalu native is passionate about cooking and a fervent fan of Maui's bounty of products from farm and field.

"I grew up with food as the center of life. From the growing and feeding of cattle, pigs, and chickens I learned about what they require to produce a quality product. From the slaughter and processing, I learned about proper handling procedures for meats. From the foods that my family cooked and enjoyed, I learned about good food, good flavors, and a respect for life."

He is a true mentor to his students and does his best to help them find satisfying culinary careers.

Pastry Chef Instructor **TERESA "CHEECH" SHURILLA** has been teaching confections and pastry at the Academy since 2001.

She has been interested in pastry since childhood. "Making apple pie with my grandma is what got me started baking," she says. She is perhaps too modest to mention that she is also the daughter of famous Maui restaurateurs Joe and Bev Gannon, who own and operate Hāli'imaile General Store and Joe's Bar & Grill.

Chef Teresa trained and worked in Europe and the mainland U.S., then returned home to Maui to serve as pastry chef at her parents' restaurants. However, she claims that "being an instructor at MCA has been the most rewarding experience I've had so far."

Program Coordinator Chef **CHRIS SPEERE** learned love and respect for good food from his childhood. He says, "I remember visiting my father's family's peach and walnut farm. Being able to pick and taste farm fresh fruits and vegetables and to experience the true and pure flavors of foods at a young age affected me greatly."

Chef Chris came to Maui in 1986 as part of the opening culinary team for the Maui Prince Hotel. He joined the Maui Community College's Culinary Arts Program in 1989. He is very proud of how far the program has come since its humble beginnings.

> "Our culinary academy is like no other in the nation. A gracious spirit exists in all we do and accomplish through the guidance of our teaching faculty. Cultural traditions are apparent in our diverse student population and our approach to multicultural cuisines. Creating a sense of place and family continues to be a most important aspect of our program and of our students' success."

Professor Emeritus **KAREN TANAKA** served as MCA's Program Coordinator from 1980-2002. Karen set the standard for excellence in culinary arts education in Hawai'i and across the nation, and it is through her leadership that MCA was the first program in Hawai'i to receive accreditation from the prestigious American Culinary Federation. Karen is still an integral part of MCA's continual development. She mentors new faculty, assists with program improvement, and emphasizes that students' success is MCA's first and foremost responsibility.

GRADUATES AND FRIENDS OF THE PROGRAM

After graduating in photography from the prestigious Art Center College of Design in Pasadena, **STEVE BRINKMAN** returned to Hawai'i where he had previously earned his undergraduate degree. In 1984, he opened his photo studio in Wailuku, Maui, where he continues to pursue commercial photography. Steve works with commercial clients in the field of architecture, restaurants, resorts, and lifestyles. He has been published nationally and internationally.

Chef **BOB CAMBRA** is a program graduate. He is currently the executive chef of The Ma'alaea Waterfront Restaurant, which has consistently been rated Maui's best seafood restaurant.

NALU CASTILLO is a former student of the program. He developed his delicious recipe for mochiko chicken when he was a student. Nalu now works at Kula Hospital, Maui Eats in Kahului, and Stopwatch Bar & Grill in Makawao.

JEREMY CHOO is a 2005 program graduate. He is currently employed at the Ritz-Carlton Lake Las Vegas Resort. Jeremy has received many MCA awards, including the 2005 MCA Outstanding Student Award, the Valley Isle Produce Scholarship, and the Kaua'i Rotary Scholarship. He was part of the Maui Culinary Academy team that won silver medals at the 2004 and 2005 American Culinary Federation competitions.

Chef **JOHN COX** is a Friend of the Program. He currently serves as Executive Chef at Ka'uiki restaurant at the Hotel Hāna-Maui and Honua Spa. He also previously worked as Corporate Chef for Passport Resorts, the management company for Hotel Hāna-Maui. In this role, he created Passport's culinary philosophy of sustainable, local cuisine, specialized in seasonal, market-based menus and designed spa-oriented dishes for Passport's properties.

RANDI CUA is a 2000 graduate of the program. He's worked at some of Maui's leading restaurants such as Mama's Fish House and Stella Blues Café.

BONNIE FRIEDMAN is a former Lecturer at the Academy. She graduated from the pastry program in 2007. Bonnie is the owner of Grapevine Productions, a Maui public relations firm. She is also a writer and cookbook editor. Her previous books include *D.K.'s Sushi Chronicles from Hawai'i* and *Hāli'imaile General Store Cookbook*.

Chef **CLAUDE GATY** is a Friend of the Program. Chef Claude was a great friend of Maui's culinary arts program during his days on the island. He was owner-chef of La Bretagne Restaurant in Lahaina. His Alsatian grandmother, who cooked in aristocratic households in France, raised Claude and imbued him with a love for French regional cooking.

CRAIG GRANGER is a 2001 program graduate. He is currently employed as the Seafood Manager at the New Seasons Market in Portland, Oregon.

Chef **STANTON HO** is a Friend of the Program. He is Corporate Executive Chef at Chocolates à la Carte, in Valencia, California. Chef Stanton is recognized worldwide as a leader in pastry arts.

Chef **LYNDON HONDA** is a Friend of the Program. He is the Corporate Chef, or overall manager, for a number of Maui restaurants and catering companies: Old Lāhaina Lū'au, Aloha Mixed Plate, Hoaloha Productions, Ho'omana'o, and Traditional Hawaiian Weddings.

CATHY NOBRIGA KIM is a Friend of the Program. She is the third-generation of Nobrigas to run Maui's own Roselani Tropics Ice Cream.

Chef **HIDEO KURIHARA** is a Friend of the Program. He currently works at the Hapuna Beach Prince Hotel. He is a master sushi chef and a three-time-winner of Sam Choy's prestigious poke recipe contest.

Chef **JAMES MCDONALD** is a 1989 program graduate. He is currently Executive Chef and partner at three award-winning Maui restaurants: Pacific'O, I'o, and The Feast at Lele.

BELIA PAUL is a 2000 program graduate. She is currently serving as General Manager of Hāli'imaile General Store (which is not a store, but a critically-acclaimed Maui restaurant).

SUWANLEE PEASE is a 2000 program graduate. She was a member of the MCC culinary team that represented Hawai'i at the American Culinary Federation National Convention in Nashville in 2000. She now owns and operates Suwanlee Catering on Maui.

Chef **ELAINE ROTHERMEL** is the chef and owner of A. K.'s Café, in Wailuku, Maui. She is a former chef instructor at the Academy.

Chef **EDDIE SANTOS** is 1995 program graduate. He is currently a Co-Executive Chef at Maui's Mañana Garage.

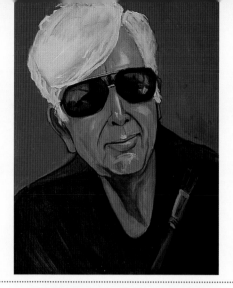

ABOUT THE ARTIST

When you visit The Leis Family Class Act Restaurant, the Maui Culinary Academy's fine dining restaurant, you will be greeted by "From Sea to Shining Sea," a gorgeous diptych painted by Maui artist Ed Lane. Ed's motto is *The art of exuberance.* When you see the diptych, or if you happen to visit Ed's website (www.edlanestudio.com) or his Wailea studio, you'll understand the motto. If you were to have the pleasure of meeting Ed personally, you'd see that the motto is doubly appropriate: Ed is exuberant in his art and in his life.

Many of Ed's paintings are Maui landscapes. Their brilliant colors dazzle; their sharp outlines and bold compositions hold the eye. They are immediately appealing.

Ed has exhibited at the Honolulu Academy of Arts and at Art Maui. His work has been shown in more than 50 juried exhibitions throughout the U.S. His art is on view in galleries throughout the state of Hawai'i, and has been acquired by many corporate, state, and private collections.

He and his wife Diane are major Friends of the Program. We are both proud and grateful that he has allowed us to use so many of his images in this book.

RECIPE INDEX

INGREDIENT INDEX

julienne, how to, 175